NEVER THIS WAY AGAIN

(Now I Know)

A Journey in Unwavering Faith

C. Beth Porter

Chapbook Press

Schuler Books
2660 28th Street SE
Grand Rapids, MI 49512
(616) 942-7330
www.schulerbooks.com

Never This Way Again (Now I Know)

ISBN 13: 9781948237109

Library of Congress

United States Copyright Registration Number TXu1-356-630

Effective date of Registration: June 05, 2007 (First)

United States Copyright Registration Number 1-6175056321

Effective date of Registration: January 6, 2018 (Second)

Copyright © 2018 Carolyn Priester (aka C. BethPorter)
All rights reserved.

No part of this book may be reproduced in any form without express permission of the copyright holder.

Printed in the United States by Chapbook Press.

Scriptures taken from the Holy Bible International Version.®

Copyright © 1973, 1978, 1984 by International Bible Society.

Used by permission of Zondervan's Publishing House. All rights reserved.

The "NIV" and "New International Version" trademarks are registered in the United States Patent and Trademark Office of International Bible Society.

Use of either trademark requires the permission of International Bible Society.

DEDICATION

This work is first and foremost, dedicated to the Author and Finisher of my faith Jesus Christ, to my children, who individually think this book is only about them, to my surviving siblings that I love with an unconditional bond, to my brothers and sisters in Christ, and finally, to the memory of the two greatest women to walk this earth, my mother and grandmother, who remain the inspiration and stronghold to and for my existence.

Since the completion of this book, my only surviving son was senselessly murdered at the hands of someone who mistakenly killed him, thinking he was someone else. It is therefore, with an indescribable grief, yet with a forever love that I dedicate this book to my son, and to all sons out there whose lives have been cut short through a wanton act of violence.

C. Beth Porter

FOREWORD

In an attempt to understand a condition that appears to have taken complete control of my every thought, this book is a narrative depicting the lives of three very prominent women who experienced a phenomenon faced by many parents; the abandonment felt when children believe their parents are no longer viable human beings that have become a burden on the lifestyles of their adult children. Being one of the three women mentioned, I would also attempt to share with you the methods my mother, grandmother and myself used to deal with this condition. I will also share with you how my mother and grandmother overcame the uncaring and negligent behaviors exhibited in their children and grandchildren.

I have yet to get to this stage of acceptance. Hopefully, what I share with you will give you the strength to let go of your perceived notions that you can handle the situation, and acknowledge that God is the only source of your strength while going through this painful period in your life. And finally, like me, may you come to a resolve even if life's outcome is not what you expected, then to find closure that is acceptable, if not ideal for the solution you're seeking.

TABLE OF CONTENTS

-Use of Scripture authorization/information

-Library of Congress: Copyright Registration

-Dedication

-Foreword

Part One: God's Renewing Strength

One:	Perceptions * Realities * History	1
Two	Shared Qualities	24
Three:	Rue	35
Four:	The Brood	41
Five:	Rue's Resale Shop	49
Six:	Journey Through Poverty	59
Seven:	Christmas on the Farm	63

Eight:	The Catch	73
Nine:	Rue's House	77
Ten:	Nino	89

Part Two: God's Unconditional Love

Eleven:	Life Before the Big City	102
Twelve:	The Town of Judgeville	105
Thirteen:	The Big City	125
Fourteen:	Retrospections	134
Fifteen:	Less Than Perfect Parenting	138
Sixteen:	Reflections	142
Seventeen:	The Other Side	148
Eighteen:	Irreplaceable losses	153
Nineteen:	Frailties	163

Part Three: Now I Know

Twenty:	Friends, We All Have Them	168
Twenty-One:	Letting Go	172
Twenty-Two:	Out to Pasture	177
Twenty-Three:	Conflicts, All My Children	184
Twenty-Four:	Children, A Gift	197
Twenty-Five:	Reality Check	204
Twenty-Six:	Resolution	214

-A Mothers' Prayer   216

-The House: Ralph Waldo Emerson   217

-End Quotes   219

Chapter One: Perceptions * Realities * History

Nino, Rue, and Cora, three women of African American descent will take you through an era in each of their times while here on earth, with the common thread bonding them together being the love for God and the eighteen children they bore between them. Now I know that only the unconditional love and wisdom expressed by my mother and grandmother through the heartache of being unneeded, abandoned, and yes, feeling unloved at times made their ability to still contribute in a meaningful way in their adult children's lives, not experienced at times by either of them. God addressed this uncomfortable period in some of our lives when He recognized this experience was and still is common among us by reminding us with this ageless saying, that's being felt by generations past and to come, "Do not cast me away when I am old; do not forsake me when my strength is gone". Psalm 71:9

Nino, full name Anna Lorraine Johnson was my grandmother; born in the "Jim Crow" era of the what was viewed by some as a *progressive* part of the state of North Carolina in the year of nineteen-thirteen, and Nino was the mother, age 13 of one son; my dad, Raymond Walters Senior; given his father's name. Nino had four siblings, two older brothers; Herman and Waldon, one older sister, Nola, and a younger sister Mary who died at birth. Nino's mom and dad, Martha and Joseph was one generation from being owned by slave traders and owners in the mid eighteen-fifties. Both parents and remaining siblings died from old age except; as stated earlier, Nino's baby sister died at birth and Nino's brother Herman died from a fire; when he went to sleep while drunk, and some burning logs fell from the fireplace onto the floor and set the entire (after my great-grandparents died) shack on fire leaving nothing but smoldering embers and the magnificent-field rocks and stones-fireplace standing.

Rue, full name Martha Ruella Davis-Walters was born about thirty some odd miles from the same *bigoted* town Nino was born in; with one big noticeable difference, because by the time Rue was born, opinions and dogmas held by some of the more passionate *dislike a segment of society* Christians, *who* wanted to be identified as anything other than someone who loved his or her neighbor? Rue birthed nine children into this world by my step-dad; Carlos Jacobs, called Mr. Jake. We believe Rue was born in nineteen twenty-five or six. No one really knows with certainty what her age was. I am worse than my mother when it comes to violating that "sacred cow" of aging which I will allow you to figure out this dilemma yourselves regarding the ancient secrets of female aging. Perhaps we will address this *ungodly phenomenon* later, if led by the Holy Spirit to do so.

My mother and dad were married one year before I was born

with everyone involved almost paralyzed with the fear of pregnancy coming before marriage, causing the traumatic and painful hypocritical behavior Nino and my dad-when he was old enough to understand-and the disguised behaviors Nino and my dad was forced to pretend wasn't that much of a big thing to have to go through; preventable. Their waiting for my arrival was the indescribable joy of Rue and Nino's existence.

Cora, full name Cora Edith Walters-Ross the eldest of four children by my dad and mom. I am not going to ask if anyone believes the same bigoted, prejudiced practices were not still in place and being practiced every day in this little, closeted behavioral town? Because in some places, these practices of bigotry and discrimination is just as rampant today as it was fifty plus years ago. I thank God for not allowing me to grow up with the bitterness some hold because they cannot or will not forgive those who mistreated them solely because they were of a different skin color? I also thank God that He (and the Holy Spirit) does not allow me to see the "color" of my sisters and brothers in Christ.

I would be lying if I said I was happy with the job opportunities, pay, and length afforded me, I wasn't able to keep a good paying job back then, but God always provided in such a way that the pain of that unconscionable treatment; of those of color, was recognized as a blessing just around the corner, but family of God, let me tell you; it was next to impossible to grasp what God was trying to teach me during that time especially while looking at those with preferential or privileged beliefs with the misguided sense of entitlement which came from; and still does in some instances even today, believing because they were the "right color" made it okay to take someone's job just because they *could*, no matter how long that job had been held by the person in that particular position. The utter meanness of this act was that in most cases, it wasn't a position really needed or desired; it was simply taken as a *show of power*. I often wonder how God felt at these times. To witness many times over the pure hatred for another human being's existence must have made God feel like He was looking at the rear end of His creation, or that of the rear of a mule.

"Honor thy Father and Mother; that thy days may be long upon the land which the Lord Thy God giveth Thee." Exodus 20:12

Now we will get into the **"meat"** of this work by referring to the above scripture from the **Living Word of God** that will give a measure of clarity to our lives. I say this because He has brought me to a point in my life where I have come, to use an old cliché, kicking and screaming with heels dug in, refusing to let go of my own perceived ideas that I have abilities to work things out for myself only to realize after many painful, unnecessary failures that there is no one or anything in this *life* to turn to but God who has promised to help us through our many everyday life experiences, therefore; until we as children of God learn this very basic truth, we will unfortunately go through many self-made trials that would otherwise be avoided if only we would acknowledge God and *His* place of ultimate control in our lives.

I have experienced the loss of many loved ones and passing acquaintances in my lifetime whether through death or simply losing contact after consciously allowing too much time to elapse between us. Sometimes the losses were simply due to not communicating with those that were significant in my life for an acceptable amount of time, or not at all, erroneously assuming "they" knew how I would feel about a certain situation which led to painful interactions with all involved. At any rate the losses experienced were felt just the same no matter who was at fault or what other circumstances were in place.

Perhaps these losses of important relationships was due to having never admitting the role I played, or if reluctantly acknowledging my role in the obvious estrangements, I did not accept my actions of not reaching out as being a part of the reasons for the losses. At any rate, God was then, and is now trying to show me and countless others that we must put our total trust in Him, even though He made us to form Godly relationships with others, we still have to remember that it is His place and not others that give *our* lives meaning and completeness. Isn't it ironic how we always look to others to validate us or to determine our worthiness? Would it not be just as easy to simply remember and rely on the promises of God that lets us know that all things are possible through Christ Jesus, and nothing of substance or of lasting value is possible without Him? I'm often reminded of Jesus' words when He said "O ye of little faith." Matt.16:8

Matthew 6: 24 states "No man can serve two masters: for either he will hate the one, and love the other; or else he will hold to one, and despise the other. Ye (we) cannot serve God and mammon." I quote this scripture only because I have come to the frank realization that there have been far too many times when I have placed my trust in *mammon,* when I *have* allowed the opinions and actions of others to serve as validation for me only to be confronted with the brutal truth that we are vastly different creations when it comes to knowing and accepting God's design for our individual lives, therefore; to seek man's wisdom is to accept the belief, thankfully shared by a small few, that man knows as much, if not more than God.

We often tend to inadvertently dismiss the vulnerability in ourselves by thinking we can renew a strength or sense of worth by subtly expecting *others* to fill voids that only God has promised He would complete in us if only we would *allow* Him to do so. I wish with sincere regret that I could boast of having the credentials that would allow me to be an expert on this phenomenon of parent-child relationships, or of having self- analyzing capabilities in place to intellectually impart wisdom to others on a grand scale when it comes to the subject I'm about to embark upon, but I only have the wisdom of God and the actual experiences of a not-so-perfect mother to share with you. However simplistic or profound, we will try to see if together we might arrive at a consensus and a workable solution to a very common, if not readily expressed occurrence in all of our lives as aging parents.

At the ripe "old" age of sixty-something (may God forgive, vanity still prevails), the mother of three surviving grown children and the wife of two deceased husbands, I find that all the sacrifices made to get to this juncture in my life have proven to be nothing more than many lessons in realizing that I still have a lot to learn. I've been accused of giving in to the empty-nest syndrome and all of the self-pitying trappings that accompany this syndrome, but am I the only one that can truly be going through this heart-wrenching phenomenon? To suffer from the "condition" of not being valued and cast aside by our adult children whether real or perceived, is a thought that is a vivid and constant visitor in some of our minds.

In retrospect, I guess it could be said that I placed too much emphasis on being the *super-mom*, and not really giving a lot of thought to what is now a confusing, delusive period in my life where reality has met me head-on letting me know that I have been sadly misinformed regarding my expectations as to how my grown children would be there for me at *all* times, regardless to how unconsciously selfish my demands were of them. Unfortunately, I was falsely laboring under self-deceiving delusions by thinking my adult children should forego their commitments to their families as expected, but; and should also honor the wishes of their aging mother (parents) instead.

These self-imposed delusions may have been my way of shielding me from a situation which I did not want to face or even acknowledge when I found myself admitting there was indeed a problem of major proportions which definitely existed in my way of thinking. If I alone "suffered" from this condition of feeling abandoned and rejected by my children, it was soon discovered not to be true. After finally opening up to several of my older acquaintances regarding what I suspected I alone was going through relating to my feelings of no longer being needed by my adult children was felt by many of them in one way or another, but anything outside the realm of my perceived ideas of what a mother and child relationship realistically should be, unfortunately had not been realized or addressed yet even after hearing the many sentiments of abandonment expressed by others. For those I confided in that had mates, the obvious estrangement from their adult children was felt with a sense of accomplishment, but for others like myself, having to go through this stage in life alone, the journey wasn't or hasn't been quite as affirming.

As I look back, at the risk of being accused of not being able to sever the apron strings (again), I have to say that my concept of how my children would later treat me is totally different from what

NEVER THIS WAY AGAIN

I am actually experiencing now. Not to say that I am now or ever was unwilling to *'sever the apron strings'* I am having to admit that it is just so darn hard when one has whole-heartedly, without pause invested so much of a personal life into the lives of others especially one's children, then to suddenly, almost without warning be rudely made aware that perhaps the way I had been looking at a particular situation regarding parent-child relationships was far from what it really is and therefore; definitely not what I had hoped it would be.

None of us as parents expect any more from our children than their unconditional love, oft times forgetting that they too one day will grow up and start families of their own which will definitely change the entire dynamics of the parent-child relationship. The role of the parent will become that of an advisor if asked, and that of the adult child; will become independence. This is what we expect should happen under normal circumstances, depending on our own child rearing skills or the lack thereof. If we fail to see this shift in the parent-child relationship dynamic, we're headed for heartache.

I might add, being "normal" the way society sees the parent-child relationship as opposed to God's "norm" as to how we are to raise our children is vastly different in most instances. Society's' secular, Dr. Spock's methods of raising children is not ideally how it realistically is or should be. Our sole desire and purpose, when raising our children must be led by God's leadings and not that of man's perceptions, rules, or dogmas as to how these paramount and tenuous tasks as parents should be carried out.

Drawing from what I feel is my paramount level of pain, also helps me realize how very much our Father God must hurt daily when we deliberately take His many blessings and tender mercies for granted. We tend to love and depend on Him *only* when things get a little rough in our lives. Have you ever given thought to God's role as Father? Can you begin to imagine the agony He suffered when He made the ultimate decision to sacrifice His own Son, Jesus Christ, to die on the cross in such a cruel and agonizing manner for a bunch of ungrateful and unrepentant souls such as some of us are, even as Christians tend to be at times? The very thought of the magnitude of that decision made by our Father God makes our little, everyday sacrifices petty and self-indulgent.

I am filled with deep remorse and shame when I attempt to think that the sacrifices I made for my children could remotely come close to the sacrifices our Father God made for us. If we could even begin to imagine the sacrifices God made through His Son, Jesus Christ, then and only then would we begin to know what it is to love so very completely and unconditionally. When and if we achieve this knowledge of God's total love for mankind, our only mission then would be to love everyone in the same undemanding, unconditional way Christ loves us.

And yet, we forget that our children are merely a loan to us while here on earth and not our personal, selfish possessions to somehow expect from them more than we are willing to give to God, because as much as we love them, God loves them more. We should be ever grateful that God knows our human frailties and fortunate for us, He forgives our acts of selfishness and childish ways when it comes to the unrealistic expectations we have in our own children.

If we have forgotten or just give an occasional, passing thought to how our Father God *also* suffered the day of crucifixion, we should revisit that horrific event when God's only begotten Son, our Lord and Savior Jesus Christ, suffered the worst torment anyone could have imagined, resulting in an agonizing and shameful death on a tree in order to free us from the foolish sin of disobedience committed by man's first parents, Adam and Eve while in the Garden of Eden. It is written, "Cursed is everyone who is hung on a tree." Gal 3:13.

Adam and Eve chose, we've come to believe, out of ignorance to succumb to the deceptions of the enemy (satan) that promised the same *deity* as God if they would commit the one great sin of disobedience which separated us from God's eternal favor by eating from the forbidden tree, all praises are to God's eternal mercies that allowed that sin and all other sins we commit today to be forgiven by that one selfless act of Jesus Christ that fateful day on Calvary.

NEVER THIS WAY AGAIN

An account of how cruelly Jesus, the Son of God, was beaten, ridiculed, spat on and mercilessly crucified can be found and depicted in vivid detail throughout the Gospels. They testify to the events that happened that fateful day and the ultimate results of His suffering, thereby being the promise of redemptive grace we received and are now enjoying as the final result of His dying for us. This was even foretold in the Old Testament when the prophets were told that a Savior would come from the bloodline of King David, and that "Jesus is the lamb of God, slain from the *foundation* of the earth" (Revelations 13:8, last portion of that verse).

Again, I could never, nor would I ever attempt to compare the sacrifices I made for my children and other loved ones to the great sacrifice our Lord and Savior, Jesus Christ, made for us. I cannot imagine, in my limited ability to minutely understand how someone could love a people that hated everything that represented anything outside of their belief system at that time, would then unconditionally love that same people enough to allow the act itself of crucifying to take place in their and future generations stead anyway? The entire act of unconditional love Jesus showed for us on the cross defies our limited, human imagination.

I am reminded of Jesus' fervent and agonizing hours in the Garden of Gethsemane praying to the Father God three times on the same evening to remove the bitter cup of death from Him, only to realize and accept that it was His sole purpose here on earth to redeem and save mankind. Jesus was finally brought to the resolve that it was ultimately the Father's Will and not His to go through the agonizing death demanded of him. (Matthew 26:39-44). This speaks volumes regarding God's infallible love for us, although undeserved a large portion of the time, if deserved at all.

Had we as human beings been called upon to act on Jesus' behalf, we would have again proven the total selfishness and self-absorbency we have sank to by demonstrating our unwillingness to challenge or intervene in what was happening to Christ. No one was willing to step up to the plate then to substitute for the sacrifice Jesus was making, and I am even harder pressed to believe anyone would today. I know God's supreme plan would not have allowed anyone to intervene for Christ, but it would have made us able to show our love for Him in a more demonstrative way in return; especially at His trial, long before He was sentenced to die. Would we today have given Him up for Barabbas? Mk. 15:15

I cannot nor will I ever fully understand the depth of pain both God our Father and Jesus suffered and continue to this day to suffer when we, His children acknowledge that *He* exists only when *we* need something. You only have to take a look around to see the unbelievably sad state we have allowed ourselves to get into when it comes to appreciating the sacrifices made on our behalf. Simply put, one would only have to look at the state of affairs in this current world system to know that we, as human beings are far from the

NEVER THIS WAY AGAIN

creation God first intended.

Additionally, when some of us fail to understand that our Father in heaven is not just *a* god that we give occasional lip service to, and realize that *He is God,* then and only then can we begin to appreciate what He has done and continues to do for us His children. In both good season and bad times, God has proven His Word by honoring all the promises made throughout time, with the death of His Son being the ultimate fulfillment of His promises. Not to thank our Father for this awesome gift, if nothing more, is difficult to comprehend. When our faith is lacking to the extent that we choose *not* to serve Him, this defies understanding, and *if* we *do* decide to serve Him, it is often on our own self-serving terms. What a Godless people, some of us have become.

I too, sometime still find myself guilty of not giving Him the praise, honor and thanksgiving He so richly deserves. I become so wrapped up in my *little* attempts to try to fix problems on my own, that I forget how very much He loves and daily shows His mercy towards us. He will not only provide for us, but our Father will *fix* those little problems that we are either too reluctant or unwilling to give to Him, again if only we allow Him to fix them for us, then and only then will we realize that a lot of our difficulties, again are self-made. Unfortunately, it is in our sinful nature to think of self first, then to think of others, and that shamefully includes God a large part of the time.

We are admonished to "Let go; and let God", but this is not always possible for me especially when it comes to my children. I won't go into a lot of details right now, but one of my children, a grown man of thirty now, often tempts me to the point that I want to ask God why He's punishing me because of the undisciplined acts of this child, but I know that God is too merciful to punish us for the lack of wisdom in our adult children, but it sure feels like it sometimes.

I also know we are never to question God because He does everything for a reason, but there is a deep desire as a mother to know *what* His will is for this young man. At this point, both my son and I are about to start questioning our sanity from the sheer exhaustion and frustration of not knowing what's next or if we should give up on one another. We wonder in our humanness, if there will ever be a resolve to the many problems he is having to go through, which is unconsciously putting everyone who loves him through torment and confusion on the same level as he is suffering.

There is, however, the comforting knowledge that God is in control of every foreseeable situation and no matter what or how He decides to address *any* given situation, it *will be* His Will to resolve the problem however HE chooses. We may not understand His reasons, but "all things work for good for those that love the Lord and are called according to His purpose" Romans 8:28. We just have to accept this as another of God's uncompromising truths.

To this day, I repeatedly find myself asking God for the same thing when it comes to my children, and that is to please **save** them. I know in my heart and through faith that we are to ask God for a particular thing and thank Him in advance for answering that particular prayer and leave it there. However, like the "heathen," I repeat my daily vigil of asking God for the same things over and over again, which must make God feel that I do not trust Him to do what I ask when I first make my petitions to Him in prayer. If that is the case *I am guilty*, but on the other hand my continued prayer is that God will help my unbelief when it comes to knowing that His timetable is indeed His and *not* mine.

I realize that I need to ask for *more patience* to wait until God sees fit to answer a particular prayer, along with the many other petitions made that go before the Throne of Grace. But again, that too is hard when I allow my worldly nature to take over where God should reign. It would be so very easy to tell you that I'm getting close to the perfection God's Word declares we should all try to attain but sadly, I would be telling an untruth. I am nowhere close, but I do try daily to reach this aspiring attainment.

Again, I know this must hurt Him deeply because as our Father, God only wants –wants, again-what is best for us, His children. Although we do not understand all that God does and why

He does them, we still have to accept His Will for our lives and know that He loves us and *know* without question that He *knows* what is best for us. We are then commanded to accept the irrefutable truth that He *is* God and that His promises are to never be doubted because as each of us should know, "He (Jesus Christ) *is* the same today, yesterday and forever." Hebrews 13:8. His *Word*, and nothing else, is the foundation for the lives of each and every one of us. God's perfect foundation has guided and will continue to guide and sustain His people throughout eternity.

As I attempt to put in writing the multitude of emotions I'm experiencing, the tears are almost blinding. Just two years ago, no one would have dared tell me that *my* children, the ones I gave up everything for, would see me suffering physically, emotionally, and sometimes financially, and do nothing except expect more from me. The mere thought of such an ambiguous idea would have been unconditionally unacceptable by me. Such an idea would have been a slap in the face *if* I had remotely entertained the thought or, God forbid, accepted it.

As stated earlier, such an observation, coming from well-meaning friends would have been in total opposition to my way of thinking. A few of these friends that offered their well-meaning, but not needed advice had never birthed a child or experienced the bonding that takes place between a mother and child while yet in the womb. Therefore; their advice was taken with little or no credence or appreciation. In other words, their attempts at *wisdom* regarding a subject *I* felt they knew absolutely nothing about, would *not* only have *not* been accepted; but would have been staunchly denied as having little if any merit or relevance to or for me.

I can't help but remember a certain friend that had a penchant for telling me how to raise my children. Mind you, Amanda although kind to a fault, would give you the proverbial coat off her back, but had never so much as taken care of a pet for any length of time. Yet I can hear her now telling me "Child, you give into them children too much, what you need to do is more correcting, and less pampering." Of course my response would always be the same no matter how often each week we had this same identical discussion. "Amanda dear, you know I love you and value your advice, but until you have some kids of your own, it looks easier from your perspective about raising children than it really is." She would always look hurt, but before I could began to feel sorry for saying what I had said, she would be off on another tangent about how I should raise my "over-protected" children.

Like Amanda's views or unsolicited advice, anything short of my other well-meaning friends total agreement with *my* perceived notion of what I thought was a perfect relationship with my children; coming from them, simply would not have been acknowledged or tolerated, *and* to the persons delivering such a contradictory message about *my* children, would have received a few choice words from me that would not have been very lady-like *or* shamefully, not that of a Christian. Looking back, I *am* ashamed of this irreverent attitude, but as always, I take comfort in the knowledge that I serve a God who is *all*-forgiving no matter how immature we may act at any given time, and He will honor our every request when we repent and sincerely ask for His forgiveness, especially when we know we are not behaving in the manner in which is or would not be pleasing to Him.

At any rate, I am now at the bitter end of reality, not knowing from one day to the next which way to turn. "But for the Grace of God," this journey into reality could have easily been a lot different than the paths it has taken me on, and the work I have taken on in writing this book could easily have been titled "The Diary of a Mad Christian Momma" instead of what the Lord inspired me to title it.

The title "Mad Christian Momma" would have been more worldly and eye-catching, capturing greater attention from the masses, and would have leapt off the bookstore shelves, generating higher monetary returns in the marketplace. However, the purpose of this work is to share a not so easily acknowledged or admitted condition suffered by most parents, mainly mothers. Therefore I will stay on the path the Lord has directed with this work so that the glory can be His and not mine in order to stay true to *His* directions.

Psalms 127: 3-5 offers this pearl of wisdom. "Lo, children

are a heritage of the Lord: and the fruit of the womb is His reward. As arrows are in the hand of a mighty man; so are children of the youth. Happy is the man that hath his quiver full of them; they shall not be ashamed, but they shall speak with the enemies in the gate." While I do not fully understand the last part of this beautiful promise, I am seeking God's wisdom to reveal its scriptural meaning as it applies to my life; in due time, as I am certain He will.

I wouldn't necessarily state that the four children I bore constitutes a "full quiver" especially when compared to my mother's hefty brood of thirteen, but four children certainly qualifies as a challenge, when it comes to interacting with that many differing attitudes and demands for individuality that each child possessed. Of the four children, each child had his or her own unique personalities. Two were the pride of any parent, having the best behavior, best grades in school, never having to ask them to pick up after themselves, not constantly bickering with their siblings unless provoked, and so on. The other two were just the opposite; which kept me on my toes but mainly on my knees *all* the time.

You've noticed I do not name these less than perfect children. They know who they are. But to be fair, I know they were trying to get my attention…maybe it was because I was seemingly giving the more "perfect" ones my attention more than they felt was fair. I felt just the opposite. God forgive, but it was almost draining at times to have to deal with the bombardment of raw emotions the two of them seemed endlessly in possession of, and had no problem with heaping their onslaughts of frustrations on me whenever one of them felt vulnerable.

I really should have gotten a degree in the elementary and middle school psychiatric discipline instead of that of a business administration major for the amount of time I spent in school seeing after one problem or another. My son, being one of the reasons for the inordinate amount of time spent in his classrooms nipping in the bud one incidence after another to keep him out of the principal's office, was always required to squelch his great need to be center stage demanding not only the attention of his over-wrought teacher, but the children in the classroom as well causing what seemed like disruption at the highest level for everyone involved. Although draining at times, it none the less required my immediate attention and on-site presence.

His unexplained desire at the time to get attention any way he felt necessary was difficult to understand before being diagnosed with ADHD (Attention Deficit Hyperactive Disorder), which explained his acting out in ways that was trying to his teachers and a distraction to his classmates, causing him to being "labeled" the class clown. School psychiatrists, after much persistence on my part to find out why my child was having such difficulties focusing on daily activities, readily diagnosed his condition as ADHD.

NEVER THIS WAY AGAIN

Never delving into the possibility that my son's inability to focus on mundane subject matter was in-part due to his being advanced beyond what was being offered academically to him, and my ignorance in believing the school system had all the answers, *and* my child's educational well-being was the school's first priority, was to my son's detriment. After being diagnosed with ADHD, put on Ritalin, and placed in a Special Ed. environment, my son went from bad to worse. But what still hurt the most, looking back was my ignorance and the inability to help him when he needed my help the most.

This is not to place blame on any one thing or persons, but it clearly shouts the need for me to have been more active and informed regarding what was happening to my child. Unfortunately, the possibilities of discovering and nurturing his creativity, and bordering on genius abilities, which allowed him to paint beautiful portraits and landscapes, to write moving songs and poems with profound depth, to be a barber that styled the latest haircut styles. and yes, to even install illegal cable, all without one day of formal training was only discovered after he became labeled ADHD and drug-addicted.

I have hesitantly shared a glimpse into my son's dilemma with you with a definite purpose in mind. The brief glimpse into my son's life is similar to that of many, but it is my prayer that parents will advocate for their children more aggressively than I did. Are any of these candid disclosures and or challenges familiar to you parents that have more than a couple of children? I will answer the question for you, a resounding *yes*, because it is the nature of the little darlings to make our lives as complicated as possible whether it be for medical reasons or by their own impish designs. If not, where would the challenge, the reward and *fun* in having them be? I don't even want to think what my life would have been like without my children. Perhaps this might be, in part, the reason I am having so much difficulty letting go.

Chapter Two: Shared Qualities

In my minds' eye, I see my mother now rejoicing in Heaven with our Father God. She was short in stature but with a presence denoting uncommon strength. She was admirably shapely yet "pleasingly plump". Her everyday demeanor was ready to go about the business of doing whatever necessary to meet the challenges before her done. She was beautiful in a universal, mother-earth sort of way, with a deep bronze-tone to her complexion, shoulder-length dark brown hair, eyes of the same penetrating dark brown that could "see behind her head" when we kids were acting up, and a personality that rivaled that of the most creative, charismatic and comedic attributes of any known personality of that day or of today. To quote one of today's worn out phrases, she was a *"Diva"* in every sense of the word, but more importantly, she was a woman of God that *lived* life as a true Christian. This is not to say she did not have her weak moments as we all do, but her way of dealing with the insensitivities of her many children and to escape from "damnation" was her uncompromising faith and trust in God.

I also see my mother, uncannily looking more like my paternal grandmother than her own biological mother, possessing the same uncompromising inner beauty and strength. Both are now deceased, but they continue to live through me. They collectively built a foundation to pattern my life after that has been tried and tested to the limit. I have religiously adhered to the values passed down and remain to this day a constant. I have feebly tried to instill the same values in my children inherited from both of them, but I have fallen short in many areas, especially trying to understand the pros and cons of motherhood and that of my mother and grandmother's seemingly effortless way of rearing their children.

Yet, while I have very large shoes to fill, I frequently have been told that I didn't turn out *too* badly. Keeping in mind, there is still this stubborn desire to never compromise my own individuality. But thank God, I have inherited the best from both of them. Those positive, God-given inherited strengths have made me the woman I am today. It is easy to recognize my frailties when looking back at the towers of strength they both were, but I am certain they had their moments of uncertainties too.

It is poignantly uncanny, but after I became an adult, I see both of them standing in front of their homes waving goodbye to me in the same disguised sadness as I hurried off to do something that I considered to be far more important than spending a few extra minutes with them, if nothing more than to just sit and admire Gods' beautiful creation with them. A cloudless sky, trees in full foliage, planted and wild flowers, the love of simplistic beauty shared by both of them. That small act of compassion and consideration by lingering a few moments more would not have been asking a lot from either of them, but at the time my priorities were more self-centered, and regrettably, less than charitable towards my mom and grandmother. My selfish and unwilling capacity to recognize the small need they both shared just to spend a little more time with me and my siblings is something I look back on and regret more than I care to admit or remember.

If only I had known then what I now know, I would have been more loving and thoughtful towards both of them and their unselfish need to just feel *needed,* while they still felt they were in a position to make an appreciable impact in my life and the lives of my other siblings, but in the earlier part of my adulthood, I have to shamefully admit that I did not give them that impression, especially when either of them would try to advise me against something I had my mind set on doing whether it was right or wrong, and in my stubbornness, I felt that I knew everything there was to know and therefore, their opinions were no more than their attempts to *meddle* in *my* life, or so I felt.

I would inevitably, always regret not listening to them because, like it or not, they were *always* right. This wisdom came from *living* life and trusting God throughout their times of difficulty, thereby learning from their individual trials and mistakes gave them the authority to impart this God-given wisdom to us. This wisdom equipped them with the knowledge to *know* what they were trying to tell us. Their unsuccessful attempts at trying to help *us* avoid some of the many painful situations and pitfalls we would inevitably face, if only we would heed to a fraction of their "brought through the fire" wisdom, fell on deaf ears. But, hasn't *not* listening been the downfall of mankind since the beginning of time? Just look back at the first children, and later, parents in the Garden of Eden.

Isn't it ironic how we overlook such little things? How absolutely amazing it would be if only we had extra sensory perception, or some inner quality that would allow us to foresee any hardships or pain *we* might cause our loved ones before it happens, thereby allowing us to avoid *all* the uncomfortable situations we may later regret because of our unintended insensitivities. My mother once said, "I hope you have two children just like you." Little did I know at the time that I would live to know exactly what she was talking about and then to pronounce the same "curse" on one of my own children was certainly not what I would have wanted for either of my less than perfect little ones?

My mom and grandmother were so much alike. They loved the same gifts God gave us in nature, the same values when it came to raising us kids, but more importantly, they had the same love for God, which ultimately sustained them throughout their lives, *and* the same unconditional love for us children, which helped them to love and forgive us despite our insensitive and sometimes uncaring behavior, which was a tribute to them in itself. They both had a certain elegance brought about by their simplistic, but robust love of life that was and is enviable by anyone so blessed to have known them.

Little did I know at the time how difficult it was for my mother and grandmother to put on that brave facade and hold back the tears that flowed freely long after one of us had left, but they did because they both unselfishly did not want me or any of my siblings to feel bad for having to leave them and go about what we considered to be our *life*. What discipline it must have taken to look at a child leave knowing that this one encounter may very well be the last. The same scenario of putting what I felt to be more important than either of them repeated itself whether I was in Michigan or North Carolina, with little or no variation.

The same unnerving encounters, but by putting on a brave front portrayed by both of them when any of us kids thoughtlessly made them feel ineffectual, is indelibly burnt into my memory, a very painful memory that I learned too well when my children would leave and I would stand at the door watching them go away not really knowing if they realized the depths of pain their thoughtless remarks or actions had caused, or worse yet, if they would even return because of some unsuspecting accident awaiting them just around the corner. I can't say with certainty if this was an ongoing, paralyzing fear shared by my mom or grandmother, but real or unreal, the thought was always there for me that any of the possibilities mentioned was a lingering concern.

My mother knew that I had a job that would not tolerate absences *or* tardiness that did not accompany an excuse from *god,* so she did not insist that I linger a moment longer than either of us felt was necessary. To quote a very touching saying and given permission to use from a friend who purchased the plaque from a *yard sale*. "People so seldom say I love you and then it is either too late or love goes. So when I tell you I love you it doesn't mean I know you will never go, only that I wish you didn't have to." The author is unknown.

This saying captures what I now know my mother and grandmother must have felt every time one of us had to leave them. I can hear them both saying as if it were yesterday "Oh, go on child, don't you worry 'bout me, I'll be fine." My selfish response would always be "ok, I would then find "something" I considered more important, like going to dinner or the movies with friends, forgetting an important date for them, but not more important than what I had to do for *me*. Now I know what it means when the bible says "You reap what you sow." Gal. 6:7.

My mother and grandmother also knew that I had a family and responsibilities that were very demanding and by that time I had been married less than five years. My first husband died suddenly from a medical "condition" the doctors flippantly diagnosed "it" as a disease of the liver, which I later learned was cirrhosis of the liver. Perhaps the doctor felt his explanation of my husband's illness was as much as I was capable of understanding at that time.

I was very young and even more naïve, and apparently ignorant regarding the doctors' opinion as to what caused his condition and I knew even less about the power we all have to *ask* our doctors questions, and not to accept their diagnosis without an explanation pertaining to a specific medical condition at face value, or if there were other alternatives that may have helped with my husband's condition, or were there options or alternative care made available to him by his doctor? These were some of the questions I later had, not just about my husband's condition and care, but to have the ability to ask questions regarding the illness, and the care we should expect a loved one to receive.

I did find out after I matured some that my husband's illness was caused by his secret drinking problem. Yes, I was very aware that he drank, but not to the extent of how much, and to what excesses he went to in order to hide his problem from me, or the rest of our families. I was angry with my husband for a long time after he died for two reasons. The first being because he was the father of my two children, I would now have to raise them alone, and the second reason being he left *me* all *alone*. I was not ready to be alone, not just because of the children but because I would now have to revert back to my mother's, what I selfishly and ignorantly called interference.

I never questioned God as to why He had taken my husband from me because at the young age of twenty-three with two small children ages three and eleven months, I knew even then that we must suffer the consequences for our foolish acts, and drinking to excess was one of those very foolish acts that my husband eventually paid for with his life; with no apparent regard for what his untimely death would permanently do to our lives.

This fact did not make me miss him any less, if anything, because of my anger, it took me longer to come to terms with his premature death. It was only after I had allowed myself to go through the normal grieving process, was it possible for me to let go some of my anger towards him, and finally start to live again. Adam was only twenty-six when he died. I later found out that there had been a long line of alcoholics or abuse of alcohol in his family.

Would I have married him if I had known of his penchant to abuse alcohol? Probably yes, because I loved him more than I loved myself at the time, another strange realization, but unfortunately true. Although not the same kind of love I had missed by the absence of my father, but a male love all the same, a love that I did not fully realize I had missed until much later in my adult life when I quite unexpectedly discovered the impact of an earthly father's love on his children. Not to be confused or even compared to the love we receive from our heavenly Father.

I still wonder today if my husband had been there with me to help raise our children, would I have over-compensated for his not being there for them by being over-indulgent, thereby disregarding some of their negative behavior as I did after he died? I will never fully know the answer to this question until I stand face to face with our Father God. At any rate, I still miss him terribly and I know our children missed their father equally as much as I did. Although my over-compensation for their every need, to excess at times, was ever present, it did not make up for the loss. Nor did all my attempts at over compensation make the loss of their father any less devastating. I had blindly hoped I could somehow fill the void left by Adam, but after quite some time it finally sank in that all the material things we may lavish on our children, will never take the place of a deceased or absent parent no matter how hard we try to cushion a child's loss with ineffective material goods.

I have only come to this realization about my husband's untimely death after much struggling to try to understand what made him drink to the point of destruction in the first place. I know without a doubt that he loved us, but in reflecting back to the time of our union, maybe the responsibility was too great for him to deal with, and maybe his secret drinking was a way to avoid the reality of being a husband and father without realistically knowing how to fill that role at such a young age himself. At any rate, I will reiterate, he not only left an irreplaceable void in my life but in the lives of our two children as well. I will share tidbits about both husbands later, but for now I just want to tell you about the two women that molded my life.

My mother and my grandmother possessed a dignity with an inbred fortitude that I can only wish I possessed a little more of. The way I see it, their lives exemplified what true motherhood should be patterned after. One of the most precious and profound tidbits of wisdom given to us by both of them was **the fact that as children of God, there was and never will be anyone or anything that breathes better than we are in the sight of God.** My mom especially loved to quote Romans 2:11 where it states God is no respecter of persons or better said, God does not show favoritism.

Although the differences in the races were never discussed with us kids, I have to believe their complete confidence in the Word of God helped them to be a living witness for us that with God's love and protection, we need never fear what mankind think or feel about us. For this, among the many life lessons they taught us, I can truly thank God that I had them as the God-fearing role models they were. I am sure that most of you feel the same way when it comes to your parents, and rightfully so, but I can only attest to the qualities I witnessed in the two women that had the greatest impact on my life; exemplified in the personage of my mother and grandmother. Unfortunately, neither shared with me the methods they employed to help them deal with the uncaring way we treated them, but I now know that their dependence on God and the knowledge that He would wipe away every tear, plus their unconditional love for us, had to have been a sustaining comfort for them, which also explains their powerful, unwavering strengths.

I still find it amazing that such an unexplainable strength was a continuous thread of empowerment that flowed throughout their lives for as long as I can remember these exceptionable gifts possessed by both of them. My grandmother often said "For every tear that falls, God waters the garden of our souls, making us stronger with each trial we're faced with." My mother shared the same sentiments, but never expressed as profoundly as my grandmother had said it.

I tend to repeat myself a lot, but I have to give credit to whom credit is due, and that is and continues to be our Lord and Savior, Jesus Christ. Without His grace, love, and daily wisdom, not one of us would be able to get through one day in this wicked, uncaring world unscathed. However, it is also comforting to know that not all the world is doomed for immediate destruction because we have someone sitting at the right hand of God, intervening and making intercessions for all of us by making it possible to be able to ward off the fiery darts from hell that the enemy assails us with daily. I *daily* thank God for Jesus and this gift.

Chapter Three: Rue

My mother, Martha Ruella Walters whom I lovingly called Rue until I was age twenty-one, chose to be called Rue because she had called her mom, Nadine Johnson by her first name shortened to Naddie, not out of disrespect, but simply because to her it was a term of endearment, so Rue in turn allowed us to call her by name rather than calling her mother. She was only seventeen when she and my dad were blessed with my birth, which might have also contributed to her willingness at the time to allow us to call her Rue instead of mother.

Everyone said she looked more like my sister than my mother as I started to get older. I often look back with fond, sometimes comical memories at how my mom would blush when asked if I were her sister, then to see her stick her chest out and proudly proclaim that I was her daughter, *not her sister*. Although she was still flattered by those "kind words," she was very determined to let everyone know despite her youthful appearance that she was a *mother,* which was more important to her than *looking young*.

As expected, this attitude decidedly changed later as she

aged because like all women we do not take kindly to revealing our age, therefore; to have *truthfully* told her age would have been in her opinion a capital sin, so rather than lie, she chose to remain silent when asked what her true age was, and no amount of coaxing or promises of elaborate gifts or money could make her reveal this well-guarded, *sacred* secret. None of us to this day can honestly say that we know her real age. She was delivered by a mid-wife, and birth records weren't accurately kept or maintained during that time, although she insisted that she was only seventeen when she had me.

She could have been older or even younger, we will never know because had we dug up her marriage license the same age would have been on that record as was on our birth certificates. Fondly, this "don't ask, won't tell" age factor is only one of the many memories of her that is still infinitely priceless and burned into my memory forever. When asked her age, Rue would honestly and innocently look the person in the eyes who had dared ask her something as very personal as her age and ask "How old do I look to you?" She knew she looked ten years younger, or had been told, so it wasn't in her opinion necessary to reveal that information to anyone. Call it vanity or simply none of anyone's business, the age of my mother remains a mystery to this day.

My mom came from a family of eight children, with both parents present in the home. Under normal circumstances, this on the surface *ideal* familial setting would have been, and should have had the ingredients that would have assured successful relationships in her adulthood with any mate she chose to spend her life with, but to the contrary. She married three times and brought thirteen children into this world. There were four children from the union with my father Raymond Walters Sr., and nine kids from the marriage with my step-dad Jacob Connors; whom we called Mr. Jake. Fortunately, for everyone involved, there were no children born from the third marriage, especially for my mother because by this time she was getting tired although you'd never be able to tell it from the way she continued to care for everyone.

Thanks to God, by the time Rue had entered into her third marriage her child-bearing days were over, also because by then; she was taking care of my deceased sister's four children and going through some trials with her third husband that bordered on abuse.

Looking back, from a human perspective, I truly cannot see how she did it, but now I know without doubt that it was God that gave her the strength to mourn Rosalind Walters-Brooks, my sister's tragic death, then to take on the responsibility of caring for her four orphaned children. The youngest little girl named Cynthia was only two years old when her mom passed. Rosalind's only son Trevor was four, Annette was eight and the oldest girl Mavis Anne was nine. This undertaking was more than anyone in their right mind would have volunteered to do but this was the kind of woman of selfless courage and endurance she was. And if that was not enough, on top of all the tragedy she had to endure knowing that Rosalind's death wasn't an accident but never voicing what she knew in her heart to be true, made having to watch her vigilantly pray for the salvation of Alonso, her third husband believing there was good in everyone, still makes me look back at her resolve in awe to see her strength in action. Tasks and challenges were becoming more daunting every day, ultimately taking its toll on Rue although she would have gone to an early grave if she thought anyone saw this weakness in her.

To try to rationalize the whys and how's Rue did all the physically, seemingly impossible tasks she performed daily, blindly attempting to understand those how's and whys only to be made aware that through the strength and wisdom she possessed and displayed, only God allowed her to do all she did. This knowledge, coupled with her unfailing faith was evidenced by the rock solid determination she had to fulfill the awesome tasks that God had given her in life, and witnessing the fact that there was nothing short of death that she would have allowed to deter or stop her from completing these tasks is still incomprehensible at times.

Something however; was amiss that prevented her from finding and staying with one mate for life, but whatever the dysfunctions were, if you can call her inability to remain in a relationship "until death departed them" a dysfunction, she chose to take to the grave with her and out of respect for her, I did not ask for an explanation because her determination and resolve to make life as kind for us as she possibly could, made not having an earthly father figure in our lives at *all* times, at least, tolerable. I can't help but wonder why my mother and father did not make a success of their marriage, but now that I'm older I can only surmise that it was because they were "unequally yoked" 2 Cor. 6:14 and unfortunately, that was and is a bad recipe for any relationship.

My only prayer is that I did not duplicate those same traits of what must look like non-commitment for the long haul in a relationship in my children, by instilling the perception or the lack of long-term commitments' as evidenced by my examples. I say this because, in my worldly way of thinking and my unsaved actions when it came to relationships with the opposite sex before I met and married my second husband, and because of the examples shown to my children, the decisions I sometimes made was not something I'm very proud of. I dated extensively, until I found Mr. Right, my second husband. I guess you could say I was on a mission to find a man, not giving a lot of thought to waiting on the Lord to send me the husband He wanted me to have.

My children saw the many men that came and left in our lives. I won't say these encounters were of the "married sexual type" relationships, but there was a certain instability present with the revolving door relationships that they witnessed that might have given them the impression that it was okay to have multiple partners.

NEVER THIS WAY AGAIN

At this time in my life, I find myself attempting to justify my every action, sometimes out of guilt and other times just trying desperately to understand where and how I went wrong, and the part I played in what is going on in my life right now.

I must say without hesitation that at no time did I give my children the impression that it was okay to be in a sexual relationship with the opposite sex that wasn't in the confines of marriage, but it probably looked that way nonetheless. I also pray that the fear of God that was instilled in them, will not allow them to use my past mistakes as a license to sin in the same manner as I did while trying to find another life-long mate after the unexpected, and short-lived marriage with my first husband. Again, the death of my first husband may have negatively colored or influenced my decisions regarding *anyone* I would have allowed being an intimate part of my life- in my then- foreseeable future. This misguided and uninformed "attitude" was unfortunate because I probably turned away a lot of good, prospective mates with the unfair comparison I made with all men that I foolishly held at the time with Adam, my first husband. Looking back, I vividly see my mistakes and grieve because now that both husbands are gone, there is not a darn thing I can do to correct my stupidity. Let this be a lesson if any one of you out there who is suddenly faced with a similar situation. Seek God *first* and He will make all things clear to you, including the choice of a husband or wife, if that is what He feels you need.

Chapter Four: The Brood

In our family, we were so *plentiful,* the thirteen of us; that today we still address each other in the "pecking order", me being number one of the thirteen, and one of my younger sister's closest to me, being number five. As I stated, we all were, and still are identified among one another by numbers one through thirteen. While there might be some in the pecking order that may resent being referred to as merely a number, that "resentment" does not take away from the togetherness and love we all genuinely feel for one another. I would be lying if I said there wasn't the customary sibling rivalry among us that was and is present in all families, but I *can* truthfully say that now, as adults; we come together in full force when our family is faced with a crisis of any kind, or to just simply get together en-masse during holidays at one or the other's homes to celebrate our togetherness.

Being the eldest of the thirteen, I do not remember having much of a childhood except for the times when we would go back to North Carolina and spend the summer with my grandmother Nino. Throughout my youth, I was too busy being a second mom to my younger siblings to enjoy my fleeting years as a child because my mother had to work to provide for us between husbands and as the oldest, the job of caring for my younger siblings fell on me, not that I'm complaining; but looking back, I longed to have the freedom the other kids in my neighborhood had that allowed them to enjoy an unencumbered childhood, especially when it came to playtime. Any attempt at playing failed miserably because if I took my eyes off one of my younger charges for a second, they would be off like wild colts. They too, probably just wanted to feel the freedom they saw the other children experiencing. An experience we both missed because it was rather difficult to get into a game of jump rope, hop-scotch, or hide and seek for the younger ones or for me holding onto someone's hand or having someone straddling your hip did not classify as playtime.

I vividly remember when other kids in our neighborhood were outside playing, although I was supposed to be playing as well, I *always* had a baby sister or brother on my hip or holding onto them for dear life. In my early teens, I was often asked if one of my siblings belonged to me. This scenario had become so commonplace on our street that everyone should have known that I had not birthed a child, but I think when the questions were asked; if it were my baby, it was just a slur intended for my mother and step-dad and their "rabbit-like" propagation methods.

Unfortunately, some of our more reserved neighbors did not believe in having more than two point two children per family, any more than the accepted number of children one should have was considered obscene by those blue-nosed hypocrites. Please forgive my intolerance with the insensitivities of those less informed than most of us, but I've still got to learn to pray for their ignorance.

I am eternally grateful to my parents for not adhering to those bigoted, uninformed ideologies. If they had, just to imagine such a family structure, leaves me with a sense of loss and sadness for all the love and togetherness from each of my siblings that I would have missed. I never cease to thank God also for the gift of a large family. We were, as we are now, a source of comfort and strength for one another. When everything in the world seems to go wrong, as it often does, we have each other to cushion some of the blows life throws at us.

Looking back, I find myself feeling anger towards our neighbors for their thoughtless remarks because like it or not, each new addition to our family is how often God blessed our family with increase, and it really should not have been the concern of the neighbors or anyone for that matter how many children my parent's had because again they weren't asking them *or* anyone else for anything. My step-dad, Mr. Jake worked long, hard hours at one of the large, then booming auto plants in Michigan to provide for his family just to prevent the ignorant gossip our neighbors were capable of, especially when they tried in vain to understand why our *extraordinarily* large family made it financially much better than most of them fared with much smaller families, most of the time.

NEVER THIS WAY AGAIN

I believe that most of the negative experiences with some of the neighbors and their less than charitable attitudes toward our family structure was the beginning of my, what I perceive now to be, false sense of pride. At the time those hurtful remarks were made, however innocently intended, I felt justified in my own mind to feel the anger as I did. I can remember telling one of the more verbal, -in your face- neighbors exactly how I felt and was in no way afraid of them or the repercussions I would face from my parents due to my "disrespecting my elders". At the ripe old age of twelve, I vividly remember telling Mrs. Fletcher, the neighbor across the street from us to "mind her old, nosy business". Mrs. Fletcher had a good view of our comings and goings, who and when we had visitors, you name it, she was the pulse of the neighborhood gossip network, and needless to say I *felt* the impending wrath of God when she told my parents how disrespectful I had been.

Mrs. Fletcher was outraged on another occasion when I told her, "if she spent as much time taking care of her nasty, stinky house and her snotty-nosed grandchildren as she did snooping into our business, the whole neighborhood would be a better place to live." Needless to say again, she did not hesitate to repeat to my parents how disrespectful I had been to her and how much more they would be able to control us bad, half raised kids if there weren't so many of us. My mom and step-dad assured her I would be disciplined for my "disrespect towards her" and they did punish me by not allowing me to watch television for a whole week. I knew my punishment was to teach me that no matter what the reason, I was never to disrespect my elders, but I also knew the punishment could have been harsher if I had "sassed" an adult under different circumstances.

In my mind's eye, I see Mrs. Fletcher weighing three hundred plus pounds; and may God forgive if it appears that I have something against obesity. But her weight stood out more than the fact that she would go for what seemed like weeks without changing out of her night clothes, hair curlers and head "rag", or bedroom slippers that she even wore grocery shopping (maybe she had a very painful foot condition), I think she did change into dress shoes on the rare occasions when she went to church. Her glasses were so thick; I don't see how she actually could *see* out of them. But again, I will not fall into the trap of talking negatively about a child of God's physical appearance and/or attributes, but I will say that when someone lives in a *"glass house"* they should not be so quick to cast stones.

I have at long last, forgiven our neighbors for their uncaring remarks and their total ignorance regarding what God had destined our family structure to be, but I am daily praying that God will not only give me patience, but also wisdom for my lack of tolerance for people that would rather find fault in another rather than try to see the purpose God has intended for the lives of those they are thoughtlessly assailing due to their uninformed ignorance.

In defense of my mother, referring to the biblical days of old, our forefathers, and the prophets, believed to have an exceedingly large family was an honor. Did not the Lord say that "Blessed is the man whose quiver is full"? I know the intent at that time was to "go forth and fill the earth", a covenant the Lord made with our forefathers, and although it did not necessarily apply literally for my parents during their time of procreation, what the harm? What is better than a home filled with children that are loved and appreciated for the beautiful blessing and gifts from God that they ultimately represent?

I can truly think of no greater gift than the ability to have children. One would only have to ask those couples that cannot have children of their own, but thanks be to God, those very couples adopt and make wonderful, caring parents and homes for our less fortunate children that are unwanted by their biological parents because of the misinformed ideas that these voiceless children would have somehow imposed an economically challenged way of life for them by their very existence. The flip side of this issue also recognizes the fact that some children were given up by their biological parent(s) out of sheer love for the child, realizing the child could not be cared for adequately in a compromising environment of either birth parent.

Rue was an unwavering advocate for the rights of children and as such, my mother was an educated woman for her time. She was a lab technician (which had no impact on her decision to become a lab technician) and was paid very well when she wasn't "going forth and multiplying". She instilled the value of a good education in all of us children, and by the Grace of God, all of us have college degrees which enables all of us to respect not only the parents' right to make informed decisions regarding their children, but to speak up for those in no position to speak for themselves. Except for my younger brother Keith, the baby of the family, who does not have a degree yet; however; he has a DB (doctorate of booze) degree that he earned from UHK (the University of Hard Knocks), that makes him the last family member to fall in line with the rest of us and our "paper" status, but we are trusting God to give him victory over his *situation* in HIS (*God's)* own time.

Also to my mother's credit, she could boast if she had lived to see it, that none of *her* children ever went to jail except that same youngest of the litter, baby brother, but thankfully that was *after* she died, which spared her from being hurt knowing that only one of us had not become what she had prayed, without ceasing, that all of us would become as responsible adults.

As stated earlier, there is still hope for this younger brother. He did finally get his GED and tells everyone he is going to go college like the rest of us did, but that remains to be seen. He still has a drinking problem that he will not acknowledge as being a problem, but there are times of sobriety when he will say that he is

NEVER THIS WAY AGAIN

tired of the direction his life is heading and sincerely wants to make a change, but again this too is only until he gets to his next drink. We all have accepted the fact that he first must really want to stop drinking, then and only then will he achieve victory over his addiction to alcohol. But more importantly, Keith has got to let God give him the victory over not only his drinking problem, but also over whatever demons that has kept him captive to this destructive behavior for the better part of his adult life.

Chapter Five: Rue's Resale Shop

We can also credit my mother for the entrepreneurial savvy that all of us have from the oldest to the youngest. I can remember when my mother was between husbands and jobs. In nineteen fifty-five, Rue discovered she could *sell* many of the clothes that she got from this big "rag" warehouse which someone had told her about; that she secretly went to mostly for us kids, for a nice little profit. This revelation was the birth of Rue's Resale Shop. Raymond and I, along with Rue would go to this huge, poorly lit, faintly musty, sometimes colder than necessary room, with gigantic bins of nothing but clothes, coats, hats, towels, sheets and other linens to find our booty for the day.

We would patiently and meticulously go through every bin in the warehouse, which sometimes took half a day or more to complete by individually going from one bin to the other to pick the very best of everything that was there with the expectation that we would make big money from the sale of every piece we had so carefully gone through that day.

The garments were surprisingly clean for the warehouse to be a place where the items finally ended up as discarded goods, but

NEVER THIS WAY AGAIN

I learned later that everything that was housed there was commercially cleaned, bundled and shipped overseas to those less fortunate than us, which we found hard to believe at the time that anyone, anywhere could be less fortunate than we were, or else, in our unspoken minds, why did we have to plough through what Ray and I considered nothing but *rags*. We quickly found out that those "rags" fed and kept us off the welfare rolls.

We would then take all that we had secured from the warehouse bins, for practically nothing cost wise, and take our bounty back to the smallest section of the two-story building my mother had rented, for less than fifteen dollars per month, depending on how many weeks was in each month and hang the clothing on racks left by the previous merchants, that the owner of the space had given to my mother, again for practically nothing cost-wise. We had no need for display cases, but we did stack wooden crates, three deep, and cover them with a solid colored sheet or very large towels to make the crates look like special display areas to place hats, gloves, shoes or any item that could not be put on hangers.

We would repeat our trek to the warehouse two to three times a week, depending on how quickly a particular item sold out. After a while, the local church members would donate dishes, pots and pans, and small appliances left over from their rummage sales that my mother had wall shelves built to specifically accommodate the storage of the regularly requested and much needed items. Rue's

Resale Shop became to the not so financially independent customer, to be what Saks Fifth Avenue is to the wealthy.

Children clothing was in particularly high demand. Finding sturdy, in fashion, kids' clothing presented a special challenge while digging through the ton of discarded "rags", but it was well worth the effort because it provided two purposes. One was a continued and much needed income for us, and the second and just as important reason being, many children that would have otherwise gone to school looking like throw-a-ways, could proudly wear clothing that was comparable to what other children were wearing without anyone ever knowing they came from a resale shop.

All the parents that shopped at Rue's on a regular basis, had come to expect only quality clothing that they could take home and launder, press, and know that their children would appreciate the clothing without questioning where their new wardrobe had come from.

I don't know how much Rue made each week, but I do know now, it kept us off the welfare rolls after my step-dad died. The shop stayed open six days a week from about ten in the morning until about six each evening. By this time the older four of us children were able to cook and take care of the younger kids while Rue worked, except for those days when Raymond and I would go to the warehouse with her to replenish the stock for the resale shop.

NEVER THIS WAY AGAIN

As always, Raymond and I would make a game of our time at the warehouse. The impromptu rules we made up helped us to pass the time through what we called "boredom". Each time the rules were different in order to keep the game interesting. "Let's see who can find the most red, short sleeved shirts today" Raymond would say. I would in turn counter and say "that's stupid, we did that last week and you won. That's probably why you want to find the stupid red shirts again, huh?" Raymond would laugh and just tell me to "decide what we would do instead."

Sundays' was Rue's day off. That was the day she sent all of us, *all* excuses barred, to church. I don't remember my mother attending church much either, but she "religiously" sent us children, even on weekdays after school, if not to practice for some upcoming special program like Easter, or Christmas, or weekly bible study, or vacation bible study, or if it would be to just simply help the janitor clean on Saturdays'. My mother wasn't raised in the church, but she knew the value of having a personal relationship with God, which was taught to her by her grandmother, and she was bound by her motherly duties to make certain that all her children were brought up in the same absolute truths of Gods' Word.

We enjoyed those Saturday's helping Mr. Franklin the janitor by dusting the pews, placing the hymnals in the compartments on the back of the pews, putting the church bulletins and items of interest in the mailbox of members, we also helped with sweeping and or vacuuming the floors, empting trash, taking forgotten articles like gloves, hats, scarves, hankies, books or whatever was left on the seats to the lost and found box in the narthex, anything that we could do to help, we would do it.

Thank God for the patience Mr. Franklin had with us. I know we could not help getting on his last nerve at times, but he had to know that our mother sent us there to get some rest from us, so I'm sure he just prayed for patience to be able to be the temporary male role model in our lives, and at the same time giving my mother a few precious moments of rest without the demands of thirteen busy, rambunctious kids under foot.

Mr. Franklin made us laugh until our sides hurt while he mocked the pastor in his more exaggerated moments of fervor. Not out of disrespect, but because our pastor, admittedly tended to over dramatize his sermons at times, thus laughing at himself at the same time, which made it alright for us to enjoy those rare, irreverent moments as well. All the jesting was done in fun and never in a blasphemous way, plus helping out by whatever contributions we made to keep Gods' house clean, got us out of the house too.

By sending us to church every time the doors opened, was letting us and everyone else know how much our mother wanted to instill the *fear* of God in us four older children. My younger siblings were along just for the sake of going "someplace" to be out of my mothers' hair for a few hours—God knew she needed the break. Having nine siblings under the age of twelve, was quite a challenge for anyone, especially my dear mother, who had worked like there would be no tomorrow just to keep a roof over our heads and the utilities paid which she gladly accepted as her lot until what she prayed would soon be some help for her in the form of another husband, but without sounding like I am vying for sainthood, being the caretaker of my younger siblings was no picnic for me or my other older siblings either, but we knew Rue needed our help and it was the least we could do to contribute to our family's well-being.

Before the death of my three siblings, by my mothers' first husband our dad, we would laughingly ask one another "when would we get a break?" Again, this was not in the way of a complaint, we simply knew that some of us may have needed a break from our younger siblings more than others, especially me, because when Rue was away running the resale shop, which was every day except Sunday, keeping in mind; the job of running the shop was also demanding. She had little time to do anything else but to stay on top of the ongoing operations of the business. As stated earlier, the bathing, combing hair, washing, ironing, and cooking for my younger siblings fell solely on us, the four older kids and back then during that time, it was a task that was viewed and accepted as normal.

By the second year of operating the business, Rue had

"hired" a couple of the moms that frequented the shop almost on a daily basis to help with the running of the shop by going to the warehouse with her to get items to restock the inventory, and assisting with constantly improving the appearance of the business which consisted of making sure that items that weren't moving, was either put on sale, or given to the church for their clothes pantry. These employees also made certain the shop never had that "cluttered" look or smell that is common in most resale shops, plus they had an ongoing responsibility to provide word of mouth advertising for the business to ensure continued growth. These tasks were something they truly enjoyed, and seemed to take pride in their contributions to the business and the public persona given off as much as Rue did.

While Raymond and I were somewhat relieved not to have to go to the warehouse and rummage through all the items there, we also felt a certain disappointment that we would no longer be able to help Rue the way we had. To contribute to the success of the business was in a way, a boosting to our egos and it separated us from our other siblings when it came to what we perceived to be the importance of the roles given to each of us by her. We felt like big "kahunas" because of our sense of importance, but that false sense of importance was snatched away from us when she hired someone to do "our" jobs. There was even a lesson in place then, but I did not see it until I became a mother myself.

All in all, Rue not only had a business that helped a lot of people, it also gave her a sense of being able to contribute again after a period of 'what will I do next' stage in her life. Although payment in the form of wages was next to minimal for her two employees, they were more than compensated by the many items they were allowed to take home after a long day's work for no charge, which was preferable to them because clothes, shoes, coats, and miscellaneous items cost more than other incidentals they had to purchase, excluding rent and utilities.

When Rue did not attend church with us, she would use the time wisely by resting up for the coming week. She truly kept the Sabbath Holy. All the cooking for Sunday was done the previous day, so we ate and cleaned the kitchen on Sundays and this was the extent of all the work that was done, except maybe going outside to play on the Sabbath; if the weather permitted, not that we called playing work, *it was work for me*. The true intent, however was to keep the Sabbath Day Holy as best we could.

We knew that God would understand if we *slipped* once in a while. If we slipped, you can rest assured it wasn't often or, Rue knew nothing about our "bending" the rules of the Sabbath, because if she had known that we willfully dishonored this most sacred day, there would have been hell to pay, but fortunately none of us had nerve enough to violate such a sacred trust, at least none of us that I know of.

I cannot and will not say that Rue was a "perfect" mother because she had her shortcomings as we all do, but on the other hand, nor can the large majority of us truthfully make the assertion that our moms are or were perfect although we would like to think so; but *I* can say, with total honesty from every fiber of my being that she was the "greatest" mother that *I* could have ever had or ever wanted.

I say this because of the true beauty and strength she exuded throughout her life, but more importantly, I am amazed with the grace and patience that was ever present when it came to dealing with the selfishness and ungrateful behavior in us, her children. I thank God she only had to experience these behaviors by only a few of us, but shamefully, I must admit I was one of the children that felt I had given enough of my life to taking care of my younger brothers and sisters, therefore, I didn't need to give anymore. But, I pray that before she died, she knew the depths of my love and respect for her, and how very sorry I was for causing her pain of any kind. **She was everything to me.**

It is only now that I have grown children of my own that I can truly respect her strength not just as a mother, but as a *woman*. For those of you that can truthfully say that you had a "perfect" mother and or father, you are truly blessed beyond measure. My grandmother came closest to being perfect to anyone I know and that is only because we *only* saw the love she showed us and never any of the pain she lived with daily, which might have given us a glimpse dimly into her humanness with its many flaws like those of my mom's that we witnessed daily, and yet knowing her strength and integrity ultimately outweighed any faults my grandmother Nino may have possessed kept her on a pedestal in a child's way of thinking.

This journey is forever a looking back at the strengths and *weaknesses* I witnessed from two of the strongest women I know. I have stated this many times thus far, but there are still not enough words to express the profound impact these women have had on my life. At the risk of yet again repeating myself, I only pray that I can have the same profound and positive impact on my children, especially my daughters again, as they had on me.

I don't know why as a mother I feel more of a need to equip my daughters with the sense and a way to express strength that I don't necessarily feel my son has to have. Yes, he must possess a strength that equips him to deal with everyday male things like providing for a family and being the covering for his wife, but most men are taught these truths and strengths by the examples they see in their fathers. Even when the father plays a less dominate role in the lives of their male children, there is still a bonding and the desire to emulate the male qualities of their fathers. My surviving son had this less than desirable relationship with his father. My husband was invested more in proving he was the greatest of providers than that of taking the time to be the dad our son needed.

Chapter Six: Journey through Poverty

My mother taught us how to "survive". This phrase is forever over used, but we could and did give a new definition to the phrase "dirt poor". This period in our lives was due to the fact that my step-dad had died and for reasons that were never explained to us, he left no insurance proceeds to tide us over until my mom found a job in the medical field that would pay a livable wage. This period in our lives was also before Rue discovered her true calling as an entrepreneur.

We could have boasted to our neighbors when they teased us about being so poor that we had not always been that way, but my mother told us that we would be "stooping to their level of ignorance" if we bragged about how well we "used" to live when her husband, my step-dad was alive. Plus, her pride would not allow her to let us or anyone else know that such ignorance regarding our sudden downward spiral into poverty had the least effect on her.

She walked as proudly as she ever had. Chest out and head held high, insisting that we present ourselves to the "tongue wagging" neighbors making attempts at trying to feign concern that was not or ever would be a part of their true feeling for us, in the same, uncompromising manner. Mark Twain phrased it with greater impact when he stated, "Kindness is the language which the deaf can hear and the blind can see." We did not experience the kindness you would expect from Christians, but we had to pretend their sarcastic and mean spirited remarks did not hurt us

My step-dad, Mr. Jake was a stern, but benevolent man that had a good factory job which paid better than average wages during the booming days of the auto industry in Detroit, this in turn afforded us a few of the extras that families with less members in them had. He tried to be the father that we needed but the stress of having to work long hours and having to be informed every ten to eleven months that he was going to have another mouth to feed, caused him to withdraw into himself when it came to interacting with one or more of us kids. He was never mean or unkind, he just simply did not have the energy to deal with any of us kids in a meaningful way outside of telling us how much he loved all of us, which meant the world to me, and I'm sure just that token of affection meant equally as much to the rest of my siblings as well. He was never a disciplinarian either, leaving that unpleasant task to my mother, who was very good at keeping all of us in line, never without love, but with a sternness that never left doubt to the meaning of the message she wanted us to understand.

Mr. Jake continued to be an excellent provider for all of us even though as previously stated, we four older children were from my mother's previous marriage, a fact that his family felt was insane when he married a woman that already had four children from a previous marriage. Until the day he died, never once can I remember him being critical or resentful for the larger than normal responsibilities he had, maybe he was just too tired to complain. I only know that I loved and respected him for being the father to me that my biological father somehow failed to be.

It is comforting to know even today that before he died, he knew how much we appreciated everything he did for all of us, especially all that he did for us four older children. He never made us feel that we were any different than the nine children he and my mother had together. He was indeed a good man and a role model with traits that I later looked for, after my "crazy" days, in the males that would become a part of my life.

After my step-dad's death, we did not know that we were anything except a large family that no longer had as many of the material things as we once had, or the "riches" our neighbors had, but we also knew *they* did not have the togetherness, the love and determination that it took to survive with as many mouths to feed, on the meager wages my mother received, as *we* did; which made our unique living situation enviable even to the more *fortunate* because everyone had to see the special Blessings and Favor that was on my mother's household. Our less than charitable neighbors probably talked among themselves wondering exactly "how did they make it" with that many kids? We later heard that some of our dear neighbors felt it was a "sin" to have as many children as my mother had. But, they will learn better when they stand before God and try to explain their mean spirited attitudes.

Chapter Seven: Christmas on the Farm

Christmas, during our time of extreme poverty was especially memorable because of the uniqueness in the way we celebrated this Holy day. We did not have money to buy gifts for one another and my mom could only afford to buy for the youngest of the children, stating that we older children knew the true meaning of Christmas and that it meant more than giving and receiving gifts. This is not to say that we did not long for that special gift that we had waited all year for, but we did understand that my mother would have done better if she could have done so. I know it must have hurt her deeply to see the disappointment in the faces of my siblings that did not get a store bought gift because they did not understand as fully as the older children did what sacrifice meant. But despite most of us not getting gifts, we still had a beautiful Christmas year after year.

Due again to the uniqueness of our Christmas', we learned early how to make decorations for the Christmas tree that we would scour our back forty for, most times coming away with a tree that had more spaces in it than branches, but after we put our garlands of strung popcorn, dyed with red, orange, grape and lime colored dried package drink mix, mixed with one cup of water and two tablespoons of any kind of vinegar for each color of drink mix used, then we would hang the popcorn up to dry after it had been strung. We had unselfishly guarded and saved the dried drink mix just for the purpose of dying the popcorn. We also used any decoration left from previous Christmas' that had survived our move to the country to decorate our tree with, which turned out to be surprisingly, a really beautiful tree. The one thing, despite our lack of money my mother would always find money to buy lights for the tree when they no longer worked and had to be replaced. Those lights for the tree for all of us, somehow kept a connection to times that were better for us financially.

Just this small jester at normalcy also kept our focus off the fact that some of us would not be receiving worldly gifts on this glorious day, not understanding fully at the time that our greater gift was and still is Jesus Christ and what He ultimately gave to us, the gift of Salvation, the one and only precious gift that has endured throughout eternity.

To celebrate the uniqueness of this day for us, we also gave one another homemade gifts which ranged from special cards with goofy poems in them, to a prized possession that we reluctantly parted with just for the occasion, but really hoping the person we gave it to, would tell us that they could not take something which was that dear to us, and therefore give it back to the giver. It worked most of the time, except for when the gift receiver wanted to let the less than benevolent giver know that they knew the true intent of their gift giving, and would keep the gift knowing that if nothing else, it would teach the giver, honesty.

During our time on the farm which was about thirty-five miles from the big city we had lived in before our journey through poverty, I can remember a brief period when we lived on government commodities. For those of you that have been blessed not to know what government commodities are, let me explain. Included in those commodities which I will tell about in great detail later, was and still is some of the best cheese made to this day. We lived on grilled cheese sandwiches at times although there was other food available to eat if we had wanted it, there was just something about that cheese which made us crave those sandwiches oozing with more cheese than necessary, as often as we were allowed to make them, providing there was enough bread and butter available to make grilled cheese sandwiches for *all* of us. As an adult today, I still crave those grilled cheese sandwiches at times, Yes, I can afford any kind of cheese I want, but nothing taste quite as good as that "government" cheese. I suppose it is an acquired taste.

In the summer time, we could always count on what the garden would provide for us, not to mention what we would catch when we went fishing. We all loved to fish, not only because it provided food for us, but we also made a game out of our fishing "expeditions" by challenging each other to see which one of us caught the most or the biggest fish. The night crawlers and leaf worms we dug from the garden or the back forty were plentiful all over the place, so we had an abundance of worms to fish with, and it didn't matter if some of the bait would fall off the hook when one of us was over exuberant when casting -with rods salvaged from our time of plenty-, but if we did run out of bait, we could always look under rocks or leaves on the river bank to replenish our supply of bait.

Unlike today where in most instances you have to pay quite a lot for bait and tackle, the ponds, rivers and lakes are carelessly polluted with chemicals from mans' "I just don't give a damn" attitude to the extent that we cannot eat the fish we catch, we were blessed then to always manage to catch more than enough fish for our supper, but cleaning our "catch" was somehow a different story. Still, those were times I continue to call the "good old days".

The fun was taken out of the contest regardless to who had won, by the fact that the fish had to be readied for the frying pan. Someone had to scale, gut and take the heads off the fish, a job *no one* wanted or volunteered to do despite the fact that everyone loved to eat their fill of the "catch of the day" regardless of the bones in many of the fish caught and the fact that not one of us knew how to filet the fish, we all became expert "fish eaters". Cleaning the "catch" was not a problem because somehow, and as usual, my mother would settle the argument as to who would do what by making us take turns cleaning the fish, and she *never* forgot whose turn it was the next time the dreaded job had to be done. Rue truly had a mind like a steel trap or that of an elephant. She forgot *nothing*. She knew exactly who did what and or when that person did it last. *Argument settled.*

Another of God's provisions during this unsettling period in our lives was that we always had plenty day old bread, pies and doughnuts that was given to us by Mr. (Elder) Willie, the pastor at the Seven Day Adventist Church who would go to various bakeries and get donated bread to give to the "poor". We were raised as dyed-in-the-wool Baptist, but my mother trusted the pastor and he was the only one that really knew the extent of our "poorness" and he was one of the few people in this little town that showed our family genuine compassion.

We would also get the bread that was too old to eat for the pigs, chickens, and other farm animals Rue had bartered for even after our "poverty" status improved and we could go to the grocery store and buy fresh bread.

We also were guilty of antics Rue would have literally killed us for if she had known about them each time we did them, and I must confess we did some of the things, like stealing corn and lying to Rue by telling her the neighbor down the road had given us the corn more than once. We weren't smart enough at the time to realize that our stories could be verified by simply asking the neighbor "down the road" if they had indeed given us the corn but we did not really get caught in our lies until my baby brother Rupert, and the oldest of my siblings Brianna, from my mother's second marriage, and myself disguised as a parked dating couple, necking when someone would drive by while the other one of us was in the cornfield stealing what we thought was sweet corn that turned out to be field corn for feeding farm animals. To our shock and amazement, all our efforts were in vain, plus we got the whipping of our lives. I do not need to tell anyone that the three of us found it easier, if we wanted corn to ask our neighbors for it rather than steal it. This lesson in trying to be clever while doing wrong became Rue's commandment, ***"Thou shalt not steal corn."***

As promised to tell you about government commodities, in addition to the *best* cheese in the world, the "monthly handouts" also included a pound of butter, canned beef, chicken, and pork, peanut butter, rice, dried beans, canned corn and green beans, orange juice, powdered milk, oatmeal and eggs, all of which either sustained us or supplemented what my mom did not have to buy to keep us fed. We were always given the allotted amount, usually about six cans or boxes of each item for a family of thirteen kids and one adult. The powered eggs used only in baked cornbread or home-made biscuits was the worst, but the powered milk could be mixed, half and half with store bought milk and it was almost palatable to the taste in our hot or cold cereals, but never to drink.

I have to admit that although we were ashamed to let our neighbors know we received government food, we ate pretty darn good most of the time. But again that was for a very short period, because my mothers' pride would not allow her to accept handouts from anyone for any length of time unless we were on the brink of starvation, likened unfortunately to the skin and bones depictions of children in third world countries. This dogged, bigger than life determination, accompanied by an almost sinful pride was also instilled in all of us at birth; or so it seemed.

My mother *and* grandmother both loved to make a garden, and from that garden they would "can" everything that was edible, storing up provisions for the winter. I have tried to this day to grow the Big Boy tomatoes they were famous for growing, the pole and bush green beans, tri-colored and white corn, okra, cabbage, collard, turnip and mustard greens, and a variety of peppers - hot, green bell, and banana, potatoes and onions like they did, but to my never ending disappointment, my harvest pales in comparison to the bountiful crops my mom and grandma always reaped.

I have tried everything I had been taught to grow a garden just like theirs but I guess my failure to do so; was in part, due to the fact that I do not use natures' fertilizer from chicken and cow manure, and ashes collected from wood-burning stoves like they did, not that I'm above using the tried and true remedies for a great harvest year after year, it's just that most of what they used is no longer available in its purest form in the area where I now live. I won't name the brand fertilizer I use, but you will know what it is when I tell you that it is a green granular substance in a yellow box. I use it for everything.

On my mother's little "farm" which consisted of five and a half acres of mostly sandy soil, but great for growing things which was a miracle in and of itself, was about three acres that was sparsely wooded, uncultivated marshy land that produced nothing more than what was already growing there, and rumored to have an underground natural gas (oil) vein running through the property. Of course all of this was rumors, first to sell the place to my unsuspecting parents, and then secondly, by my mother in order to keep the home in our family to pass down from one generation to the next, but this was not to be because less than a year after my mother's death, the home was sold because no one wanted to be responsible for the taxes which we found out was more than four years behind.

All of us could have gotten together and paid the back taxes, but there was a feud brewing between my two younger sisters as to who would actually take ownership of the home, which left us, the older four of the children out of the equation because our step-dad had purchased the home. This is another time I am relieved that my mother was not here to witness this division, and as the oldest, I am truly ashamed that I did not intervene in time to prevent the loss of something my mother had sweat blood to keep for *all* her children.

Meanwhile, back on the farm when things had finally gotten better for us financially, we acquired more chickens, ducks, pigs, a goat and a cow to add to the few scrawny chickens we already had. The cow and the goat were just for "show" because neither gave milk and neither was butchered for meat, but all of the other farm animals were fair game. To have just one cow or goat meant that things were looking up for the owner of such a rich bounty, so I guess you could say that we were finally moving out of our poverty status being as we had both a cow and a goat. Would this also mean that you had *arrived* if you owned a horse and more than one cow and or goats?

The farm animals continued to be fed with the older than day-old bread (mixed with water or mixed powdered milk, mostly water) that we without fail got from the Seventh Day Adventist pastor. My mother was always "investing" in livestock, but sometimes if that were possible, she would invest too much. Customarily using the bartering system, she acquired a sizable menagerie of farm animals. The old bread was a lifesaver thereby, never causing a hardship on us to keep the animals fed when my mother could not buy "animal food" that contained the needed nutrients not found in the bread alone for the animals to eat.

We fed our two dogs, Jack and Sam from table scraps when there were some left, but most of the time they had adapted, out of necessity to eating the day-old bread like the other farm animals. Jack and Sam were given to us as pups, so they adapted to circumstances as if they were one of us, and sometimes you would think they were human just by the way they assumed their positions in our family. Jack was a German Sheppard mixed with God only knew what, and Sam was a Cocker-Poodle mix, but they both were fierce protectors of our family and no one got too close to any of us unless either of them knew that particular person. They both are in doggie heaven now making someone there as happy as they made us while here on earth.

    Thank God He mercifully brought us through that very uncertain time of not knowing from one day to the next where our next meal would come from, at the darkest hours in our lives with the awareness that everything we went through was to build our trust, and a richer and deeper faith in our Lord and Savior Jesus Christ, and to make us fully aware that He alone was able to touch the hearts of His servants here on earth to help us through the insurmountable odds that were against us during the depths of our poverty. I am reminded of an old quote by an unknown author, which states "Where the Will of God leads you, the Grace of God will keep you."

Chapter Eight: The Catch

In my mind's eye, I can vividly see my brothers while on the "farm" chasing a young chicken *or* an old hen. They didn't know the difference (and neither did we) because they would simply catch the first thing they could get their inept hands on. My mother only found out whether it was a young fryer or a roasting hen when one of my brothers would bring their "catch" into the kitchen *or* unfortunately, only just before Rue started cooking the bird, but prior to this, your guess would have been as good as hers as to the tenderness of the bird. During the early stages of our "poorness", the chickens they were chasing was so scrawny, it was hard to tell by the best of chicken breeders how old any of the birds truly were. It was indeed a challenge to figure this out prior to the bird making it to the cooking pot.

Before taking the chicken into the house, my brothers would then have to decide among themselves who would "wring" the chicken's neck, and who would "pluck" the feathers from their catch after getting the boiling hot water from the kitchen my mother had gotten ready in anticipation of their successful conquest to get the chicken ready for baking, frying or stewing, depending again on the tenderness of the bird. They would always arrogantly state that they had caught the chicken, and why couldn't one of us girls clean the "dad burn thing". Incidentally, that was the *only* way they cussed in front of my mother and got away with it. I am quite certain their profanity consisted of far more colorful words than "dad burn" out of our mother's hearing range.

Their stumbling over one another while trying to hem the chicken up to catch it was truly a sight to see. It took about four of them to catch *one* chicken. When the task was finally done, after much cussing that they dared not let my mother hear, and falling over one another sometimes having the bruises to prove their haphazard approach to "cornering" the chicken, they would have mud and or grass stains from head to foot and a chicken that was probably more relieved to be finally caught than to have to keep up the hectic "guess who will catch the chicken" game that had gone on for hours, or so it seemed, with the chicken *choosing* to be caught instead of suffering the agony of putting up with the bumbling antics of my four brothers any longer.

This scenario was repeated each time they attempted to "catch" our supper. One would think that after numerous successful conquests, they would finally know how to be more efficient when catching a chicken. It wasn't because either of my brothers were lacking in the brain department; in fact they were very bright, they just loved to play, and unfortunately they turned everything into a game, including catching chickens. I might add that although not by choice, we could have been labeled "vegetarians" long before the choice in our habit of eating meat and fish were popular, if left up to them and their skills at catching the meat we had for our supper.

Can you imagine what would have happened if they had had to catch more than one chicken for our supper? It scares me to this day to imagine the chaos that could have ensued. I am also still amazed at how my mother could stretch one chicken to feed all of us at any given meal but she did, and believe it or not we all had enough to know we were eating chicken, but I would be lying if I said that we knew what a whole piece of chicken looked like before we got grown, but we had such a large variety of other foods my mother would prepare so that we would all leave the dinner table with our bellies full.

It was also a blessing for the pigs that my brothers never had to slaughter them. I can't begin to imagine all the mishaps that would have taken place if that job had been assigned to any one of them, meaning my inept brothers. Thank God we never had to find out, due largely in part to each neighbor at that time, despite their duel personalities, would slaughter a hog or cow, and everyone would share with one another. This ensured that everyone would always have fresh meat during slaughter time, whether they liked one another or not. It was the "Christian" thing to do. They would tell themselves this after they had mercilessly talked about the very neighbors they were sharing with. I have not learned yet how to deal with such blatant hypocrisy, but I am learning with a lot of prayer for patience with them and then, wisdom.

However, looking back there was one time my brothers were asked to catch *three* chickens for a Sunday dinner my mother was preparing for the "Baptist" pastor and his wife. Rue somehow, for reasons none of us understood, wanted to impress the invited guest. Plus she knew the pastor could eat a whole chicken -no lie- by himself, which was the reason for challenging my brothers beyond their normal one-catch *expertise*, but the results were so disastrous that my mom decided to only make *that* request on the "rarest" of occasions for fear that one or more of my brother's would really hurt himself or one another to the extent that their injury might require a trip to the emergency room, which she simply could not afford, especially when the injurious accidents were caused by their boyish rough-housing.

God was there then, as He is *Now*, I've just got to acknowledge, claim, and honor this unquestionable, irrefutable truth. Our overcoming the depths of poverty as we did only made us realize that God would never test any of us beyond our level of endurance. He is faithful to see us through each and every hardship, with the promise of a rich Blessing at the end of what may seem like a never-ending life of trials and tribulations. For this I am truly grateful.

Chapter Nine: Rue's House

I recall a certain day in particular, when my weekly weekend visit with my mother was coming to an end until the following weekend, but this particular "goodbye" is one that is burned into my soul. By this time, all of us kids had a "life" of our own, with families and jobs that we considered to be the norm without college degrees at the time. Most of us were still either finishing or pursuing our higher educational goals in addition to working and raising our own families. I had promised Rue on that day that I would buy and bring two purple rhododendrons on my next visit to plant on each side of her front door, but because of what I felt at the time to be life's hectic demands, I was prevented from honoring this very small promise, or at least it seemed small to me but needless to say, that promise had giant meaning and implications for my mother.

She felt this small addition of Rhododendrons would not only add beauty to the front of her home, but the purple Rhododendrons would add a certain touch of "class to her palace"…she laughingly stated. We all inherited her sense of humor, a gift that has gotten me through a lot of difficult times. I am sure, without her sense of humor, my mother would have given in to the hardships that were ever present in her life for as long as I can remember. I now know that those rhododendrons represented more than a dressing for the front of her house, but she played it off to be no more than just that, stating it would add class to something that she had accepted as her lot in a soon to end life.

There was no traditional porch, just a large concrete slab that served as a front porch that led to the entrance of her home. After my step-dads' death, with no insurance to provide for all us kids, we went from a two story, five bedroom, two and a half baths, finished basement with recreation room, home to a two bedroom "sardine tin" of a house with no running water and a bathroom toilet and sink that did not work most of the time when the home was first purchased but later fixed to be a functional, beautiful room. Rue continued to live in her miniature "palace" after all of us had left to make homes for ourselves and our families.

This home had been purchased a couple of years prior to my step-dad's death specifically as a fixer-upper to either sell or use as a weekend get-away in the country for my parents in their declining years, but never as a home for our exceptionally large family. The house was not designed for that purpose. Little did we know during our time of "more than enough" that one day that very house would become a lifelong character building experience for all of us?

The old woman in the shoe had nothing on us. With six brothers and six sisters, sharing one of the two moderate size bedrooms, the sleeping arrangements bordered on miraculous. There were two sets of bunk beds, one set for the boys and one set for the girls. It was up to us who slept at the head or the foot of the beds each night, when I think about it, it really didn't matter which end we slept at because we would still have someone's foot in our mouth or across our back or chest depending on what position landed in after finally passing out from the sheer exhaustion of having to make such a paramount decision about who would sleep where.

Needless to say again, most nights we fussed about this arrangement until we finally passed out from sheer exhaustion only to have to get up "with the chickens" the next morning to do the numerous chores assigned to us before we either went to school or, to start our *many chores* and our imaginary adventures in the summer when there was no school. Unlike the time when we lived in the city, we actually had more freedom to be kids because the younger children could be allowed to run "wild" without causing problems for our intolerant neighbors.

The home, in spite of its many shortcomings was what we lovingly called our "cracker box" house that was unusually well insulated; despite its other needed repairs, which helped to keep it warm (or was it the body heat from all the people in that tiny little house) during the colder Michigan months. The house itself was constructed using concrete or cinder blocks, with walls of cheap plasterboard. Not knowing much about insulation, I do know that much had to have been used, perhaps in places not usually designed for insulation in order to keep the house as warm as it stayed during the colder winter months.

We did manage to keep the propane tanks filled in the winter months to keep warm but, due to the blessed fact that we cooked on an electric stove, we did not have to worry about keeping the tanks full at any other time because we could heat water to take baths on the kitchen stove. On the down side, we did have to go a quarter of a mile to a spring in back of our house, or the town hall to get water from an outside faucet until the councilmen decided that it cost the township too much to provide free water to its residents. We had to get water for everything, drinking, cooking, bathing, and flushing the toilet until we got the water line ran from the road to our house which took an inordinate amount of time to get done because of township legal red tape regarding zoning laws, but after about six months of pure torture by having to haul tons of water and seeing the pointing fingers and snickering by the more fortunate passers-by that had water lines running to their homes, Thank God we finally got running water in our home as well.

The bathroom and all its fixtures was the *first* repairs God blessed us to get done in our humble abode. It had proven to be disastrous when we did not have a working toilet for all of us in that one bathroom home. Can you begin to imagine how much water we had to haul, before we had running water, just to keep the toilet flushed? A lot of us, because of necessity would have to go out back to use the bathroom in what we affectionately called our "back forty". We always prayed it would be before dark when nature called because we were afraid of all the unseen, creepy crawlers that might jump up and bite us while we were in such a compromising position.

We were at the laundry-mat every other day until someone anonymously put an old wringer washer that still worked on the side of the house under our covered breezeway, which led to a lean-to shed we used for storage. Whoever gave us the washer was even thoughtful enough to put it in a place where it would not be exposed to bad weather until we were able to take it into the house. What a God send. We reveled at the thought of not having to take the ton of dirty laundry, to be stared at in amazement by the other patrons of the laundry-mat every time we went there. It would cost my mother almost a day's wages to wash all the clothes that needed to be laundered for fourteen people, and this had to be done at least twice a week despite the fact that we all learned early how to wash out our under garments and socks by hand, which saved a tremendous amount of money each time we went to the launder--mat.

We still had to use that beautiful old washer just as often as we had done when we went to the commercial clothes-washing establishment, but we did not care because with the exception of having to risk getting our fingers caught in the wringer, and laughing our silly heads off looking at how flat whomever fingers was "squeezed" in the wringer was, that washer was a welcome addition to our mighty brood and we thanked God each day for the person who thought enough of us to give us that beautiful gift. Incidentally, it still baffles me as to how someone could have left something as large as a wringer washer without anyone seeing him and/or her do it. Whoever our benefactor was, they had to have delivered the washer at night when everyone was sound asleep, but again, thank God for them and the much-needed gift. We always speculated that it was the Seven Day Adventist pastor or one of his members that blessed us with that washer, but the identity of the person was never known to this day and we did not ask.

Each child had their own personal space at Rue's to keep our clothing, books and any "valuables" we might have acquired. Each of us had the usual items of clothing, shoes, coats and hats, our own individual collection of "art", usually pictures of our favorite pop artist, "stashes" of makeup kept by us girls, secret love letters hidden in the diaries that no one was supposed to know about, but read on a regular basis by *everyone,* and the usual treasures that boys refused to live without, e.g., the rare Green Hornet, Batman and Superman comic books, the cat's-eyes or multi-colored large shooter swirl marbles, and let's not forget the occasional frog or baby snake they would sneak into the house without mom knowing about it until one of us girls, petrified, ran screaming to momma to "squeal" on them hoping they would get the worse "killing" of their lives, whoever the guilty party was we did not care, we just wanted them to pay for scaring the crap out of us. I know some of these incidents had to tickle my mother, but not once did she minimize how we felt when we told her we had been *victimized* again by our brothers' cruel tricks.

By and out of necessity, I truly believe that from that tiny seed planted "to keep *everything* in its place" or was it from our being so poor could it have possibly started the beginning of my "pack rat" *ailment?* I save *everything*. Because of this "ailment", I thank God my children have vowed not to be like their mom when it comes to an "almost" being guilty of hoarding things "condition". Fortunately, all my children seem to have an aversion to saving anything that is not of immediate use, which may be good to a certain extent, but sometimes they tend to be wasteful, which in my opinion is just as bad as hoarding. I am praying for a balance in their lives when it comes to the extremes they have taken in their avoidance of becoming a "pack rat."

The floor at our humble abode was no stranger to any of us either because after the large sectional sofa and all the chairs in the living room and those also from the kitchen had been occupied, the rest of us made ourselves comfortable any place on the floor we could find to get a good view of the one television set we still owned and whatever program, usually cartoons, that was on at the times my mother allowed us to watch television.

One would think with that many people in such small quarters that "messy" and "cluttered" would be a kind way to describe the appearance of our house, but *my* mother "adhered" to the expression "cleanliness is next to godliness." How was this accomplished? My mother believed in <u>*not sparing the rod*</u>. Each of us learned early the meaning, and the reality of that phrase.

Good or bad, right or wrong, however we individually choose to discipline our children, I thank God for the instructions (and the rod) I received from my mother for it taught me valuable lessons that I would not have learned from a more "liberal" parent when I strayed onto the forbidden path at times during my formative, or should I say *explorative* years when, not unlike many young women during what I called my "repressed" time, my curiosity had peaked, and I was chomping at the bit to find out, in a hurry, all that life had to offer. But for the Grace of God, and the *fear of the rod*, I was spared a lot of the crisis' that would have been inevitable had not the restraints been there which prevented many of the mistakes I would have otherwise made.

On the day I mentioned earlier, mom and a friend, Miss Macy were sitting out front; on this god forsaken, discarded car seat someone had salvaged from the back of an old 1939 Buick that had been junked in our next-door neighbor's backyard, but "very comfortable" my mom would tell us, enjoying the sun. By this time, contrary to the way we were brought up, my mother had a knack for "collecting" things that we all felt were unnecessary, not to mention, unneeded. Without reservations, she could have afforded any outdoor furniture she wanted, or one of us would have gladly bought some outdoor furniture for her if we had thought for a moment she would have accepted it. She did not want to feel she was a burden on us, so she never really asked any of us for anything, and would get madder than a wet hen if we insisted on doing something for her, which she was determined to do or buy for herself.

As I was leaving, she looked at me, eyes misting, desperately trying with much difficulty to hold back tears and said, "It is so good to see you come, but so very hard to see you go". The inner conflict I am now feeling is a combination of guilt for realizing that I could have been more receptive to her inner struggles, and for not genuinely being in tune with her real emotions, plus I am feeling deep remorse for the insensitive way I shrugged off her apparent need to connect with me emotionally enough to share the fear she was experiencing due to the anxieties about her not to distant demise which was ever present with her, but not shared with any of us.

The statement about not wanting to see me go would not have had the impact, which it later had, but shortly after that visit, the cancer that she had cleverly kept from all of us, took a turn for the worse and she died about a month and a half after that. We knew that she wasn't the same feisty, fire-spitting dynamo she had always been, but we chalked it up to her getting older and not wanting to let *any* of us go, this is not to say in hindsight that she was unable to sever the apron strings either, but she did seem unusually sad when one of us had to leave and go about the living of our own lives.

Now I know that her sadness and the desire to keep each of us with her as long as possible was because she knew that her time wasn't long here on earth, and our nearness, ever so briefly, to her would somehow cushion the uncertainty, and yes, the fear of the unknown which had to be unnerving even though she was confident that when she left here, she would be with the Lord. Having this incredible knowledge that we will ultimately be with our Father God when our time is up here on earth is a great assurance, but to be able to share our going away with those we love the most is also a remarkable and great comfort, but to be able to share the reality of our own immortality with loved ones, also adds a certain measure of acceptance to this inevitable time in all our lives as well.

I'm still beating myself up on a daily basis because I only wish I had known, or more importantly, that had I taken a few extra moments to allow her to tell me what undoubtedly had to be, if not tormenting her, being of great concern, perhaps I could have made the impending journey home a little less lonely for her. Now that I think back, as I remember my last times with her, I really don't think she would have shared that she was dying from cancer, because her pride would not allow her to be pitied by any of us, nor would she have wanted any of us to be prematurely saddened or have our lives disrupted because of her "I'm not ready yet" death sentence, but she *would have* "prepared" us for her death by giving us certain scenarios, if she were to die tomorrow, what would we do kind of questions, which was her way of sharing what would not allow us to treat her in a pitying and condescending sort of way.

All of us would visit her on a regular basis, but now that I look back once more, it was more out of obligation than really wanting to spend time with her, our lives were just taking on meaning, or so we thought, which selfishly gave us license to ignore the pain and disappointment she was experiencing, but so very cleverly concealed. She never complained but I now know she was hurting deeply with feelings of no longer being useful, not to mention the fact that as we found out later, she did not know how long she really had left, although her every action spoke differently.

Rue's doctor told her she had six to twelve months left, but the cancer spread so rapidly, that less than two months after the earth shattering diagnosis, she was dead. That among other situations I vividly remember, exemplifies the pillar of strength that my mother was, and it is a trait and a strength that I try to emulate daily.

I was "too busy" to buy the rhododendrons I had so faithfully promised her, so she was never able to see them planted by me at her doorway. I sadly find a strange comfort in knowing that where she resides at now, I believe there must be a variety of every rhododendron God has made. Purple ones, pink ones, blue ones, white ones, a whole forest of rhododendrons, and they're all just for her. Praise God. She doesn't need to add "class to her palace" because the palace she now occupies has every amenity provided by God, which challenges the imagination to fully appreciate its beauty and awesomeness.

Yes, she is in Heaven now, and I am confident that even there she knows that I love and miss her desperately, but it would have been so much kinder to her, and I would now feel less guilty had I shown her that I loved her more while she was still here with us. My unconditional love for her, had I expressed it to her before her death would have made a world of difference not only to her but to me as well, thereby easing some of the remorse I feel for not showing her my love. Instead I settled for telling her and making empty promises about what I was going to do to make her happy, *one day*. All thanks are to God our Father for filling the void in her that we, her children were too thoughtless and self-absorbed to acknowledge.

Chapter Ten: Nino

My grandmother, Anna Lorraine Johnson, we called her Nino, had an equal impact on our lives, especially mine. We spent many of our summers with her after we moved to Michigan when we were very young. We, meaning my sister Rosalind, and brothers, Raymond, named after our biological father Raymond Walters Sr. He was Raymond Jr., but if you wanted a fight on your hands call him Junior. I think that the designation of Junior somehow took away from his identity as an individual. We just called him Ray it was a lot safer. Rupert, a name he vowed to change immediately when he got "grown", was the youngest of the four of us and he was named after a great uncle on my paternal grandma's side of the family. I don't know to this day who Rosalind was named after, I think my mother just liked the "air of distinction" the name somehow exuded, and gave it to her. Anyway, that was the order age-wise for all of us from my mother's first marriage. I am the oldest of the four siblings, named Cora Edith after Nino's grandmother.

I truly cannot remember a happier time than when we stayed in North Carolina with our Nino. I challenge anyone today to live through the hard times she endured and not become bitter or just give up under the strain, but she persevered beyond what I could have realistically expected anyone to overcome and remain sane under similar circumstances, but I guess, no; I know that this again is and was the strength she possessed that comes only from a loving God.

As children growing up around her we weren't privy to the side of her life that allowed one to glimpse into the raw pain she felt daily because of the hateful remarks and dirty looks she got from a people that was guilty of far more than what she was being ridiculed for. We only saw the positive images she projected rather than what she was really going through. I later found out that she had my father out of wedlock, which was considered "disgraceful" during that time in our past, not because it had not happen before, or wouldn't happen again, and again, but it was frowned upon in the little close-knit, nosy, and self-righteously judgmental town she lived in by all the self-righteous, do-gooders there.

Again I will state that her plight was more common than acknowledged, but because all such "carrying-on" by others who blindly denied that such indiscretions were going on, hid their "mistakes" and "it" was never talked about or publicized. Their little secrets either went to live with a relative in another town or state, depending on how well the secret was to be kept, or the young women went to an unwed mother's homes that no one was supposed to know existed; or so they thought. It was always stated that the girls were away "visiting" a sick aunt and *their* "secrets" went into an orphanage to await adoption. At any rate, the problem remained a well-guarded secret that fooled no one but the ones trying to hide their *own little, hypocritical indiscretions.*

Burdened with the task of raising her son alone, without the financial help or moral support of her child's father, which was one of the many reasons keeping a child in those days was frowned upon, not to mention having a "bastard" child was just simply not done without suffering every form of disgrace. Any act of kindness from her parents towards her was not given because one might perceive such support for her and the child to be a way of condoning her wayward behavior, making their much needed support for her not there either. After all, *their* daughter wouldn't dream of having a child without the benefits of marriage. I do not personally condone the bringing of children into the world without the benefit of marriage either, but who am I to judge. Jesus would always ask those **without sin** to cast the first stone. I probably won't be throwing stones at anyone, any time soon, if ever.

Nino never asked anyone to feel sorry for her, she was also a very proud woman, but to be ostracized by her equally self-righteous parents was indeed quite the burden to bear for a young mother during that time in history. Nino was only thirteen when she was, taken advantage of by someone much older and wiser if you can call it wise to sexually take advantage of a child, but this was something I am told went on rather frequently; which in my opinion should have been considered when a young girl came up "ruined." I find myself getting very angry just thinking about the double standards, which were in place during such an *unfair* and *unjust* period in our history.

I am sure Nino spent many a night crying and longing for the man that had sweet talked her into doing the "unforgivable" with the result of that one nights' torrid "love" affair being that of no more than a life of shame and regret for the rest of her life. Except for the joy she found in the beautiful, unconditional love she shared with her son, nurturing him and trying to make up for the father he would never know, which was an agreement made out of a selfish demand from the father, she accepted her plight. She was resigned to her lot in life to be that of unmarried loneliness, and outside of God she found whatever comfort there was to be found in that meager existence.

While her son, my dad was growing up, she showered him with so much love and attention he did not have the occasion to miss his dad, but I am certain that as he got older, there had to be questions about his father that he didn't dare ask his mom for fear that she would think that he didn't love or appreciate all of the sacrifices she made for him. Sometimes I don't understand why such an important fact should be withheld from a child, but I do understand some things in our lives can be so painful to talk about that we just conveniently forget them or choose not to discuss the situation at all. Sometimes it is better to leave skeletons in the closet if we know that revealing them will cause more harm than keeping them a secret. She lived with the disgrace of her "mistake" daily, with only God and her son as a source of strength and comfort for and to her until her *precious* grand children came along.

We spent a couple of winters with Nino also, and even though we had to "tote" wood to keep the wood box full for the stove that was used for both cooking and warmth, and tote water from the spring for all use before the pump was installed in the house, she made the chores seem like fun instead of the drudgery that I have now come to associate with those times. There was an old abandoned saw mill a couple miles from Nino's house, "way back in the woods" we used to say, that all of us would go to and pick up discarded pieces of wood left by the loggers. Nino was very creative. She would tie an old wool blanket on both top ends with a rope and place the wood on the blanket and drag it back to her house. If we didn't find a lot of wood that day, we all would take turns riding back on that "magic carpet."

Like the teachings of my mother, during the summer she taught us how to plant, weed and general cultivation of a garden in order to reap a maximum harvest. She taught us how to use ashes from the stove as fertilizer, as well as cow, chicken, and pig manure for her vegetables as well as flowers and shrubbery plants alike.

My mother used everything my grandma used for fertilizer except the ashes from a stove in her garden in Michigan, but on the other hand, while my mother did not have a wood-burning stove, she had the farm animals that my grandmother did not have. In spite of their disdain for my grandmother, Nino would get additional animal manure from her farming neighbors and most times she would have to pay someone to bring the "fertilizer" to her, or go and get it herself. Their hypocrisy still ran deep. I'm not sure dung collecting is a job I would have enjoyed doing, but with all the minor exceptions which had to be considered for the growing strategies used, the results were the same come harvest time year after year big, bountiful vegetables so plentiful, the non- gardening neighbors could reap the benefit of my grandmas' labor in exchange for the "fertilizer" they had provided her with, (even the ones that charged her) at no charge to them.

My mother and grandmother just had a knack for growing things, regardless of the special, yet sometimes peculiar little techniques they used to achieve the task of having the best garden in their town or city. In other words, their gardens year after year was a wonder enviable by many want-to-be expert gardeners to this day, if they were still alive. My grandma and my mother learned their gardening techniques from their mothers, and the tradition went back as far as either of them could remember.

Some mothers teach their daughters how to cook, some teach

them how to sew, knit or crochet, while some mothers teach their daughters the art of being good wives by being submissive, but my mother and grandmother were taught how to provide for their families by gardening, then canning their harvest, and finally, year after year, just stepping back and enjoying the sight of all the jars lining the many shelves for future use, knowing they had accomplished a very tangible need to feed their families. This is not to say their mother's did not teach them other skills necessary to succeed in life, but "growing" things was an art, in their opinions, worthy to be passed down from one generation to the next. As told earlier, to add to the traditions passed down, I don't know from whom my mother learned her business savvy, but she passed this valuable knowledge down to each of us kids.

As children we never really gave much thought to how resourceful the use of "natures" fertilizers were, but I now know that everything grown at that time was free from all the chemicals and preservatives that are found in our daily consumption of foods grown today and far more healthy for us, but to our disadvantage, the old fashioned way of doing most things are now pooh-poohed by the younger generation of today. Sometimes, it would behoove us to recognize and appreciate the values of yesterday as wise counsel for us to live by today.

Although everyone seemed to have died at an earlier age during my grandma's time, they did not suffer with the many diseases we have today, or to complain of the massive number of illnesses suffered in today's society. Could this in part be because everyone had to do more physical labor then than we do today with all the technological advances we have that keep most of us in a sitting position for long periods of time, day after day, has this caused or contributed to our current medical woes, or worse yet, in days past, was all health care being performed by country doctors that had to take care of so many people that by the time he, usually a man, or a midwife got to someone critically ill they were on their death bed, and in most instances, it was just too late? It gives us something to think about.

Thank God for the advances in medical science and an abundance of doctors of every specialty or discipline that allows for treatment that prolongs our existence here on earth; that is, unless we live too long, which seems to be viewed as a curse rather than a blessing for those who have to give up their valuable time to take care of an elderly or aging parent, or for the one that more importantly has to give up their independence due to advance age, being made to feel that they are a burden, if not on their immediate family, on someone in a health facility that view their jobs and a pay check more important than the person they are caring for.

The most memorable and life sustaining gift Nino gave to us was the precious time we spent at her knees listening to her either read the Bible or tell us stories, as only she could, about Jesus and what He did for us on Calvary. We especially loved to hear her tell the story of Jesus' birth. She had a way of making us feel that we were right there in the stable on the night He was born. We heard the sheep bleating and the cows lowing, we smelled the frankincense and myrrh. We felt the straw which carpeted the stable floor and padded the drinking trough used for the manger. We also smelled the crisp night air that caused us to shiver just from the descriptive way she told us about the stillness, yet anticipatory air of expectation present. We saw the star the led the wise men to the baby Jesus, we saw the entire manger scene as if we were really there just from the illustrative way she told the story.

Nino would also tell us that we were "living in the last days." I, many times thought that the *end* had really come when the sun was going down just before dusk, it would be a bright orange, which looked like it was on fire to me. I found it very strange that this full, blazing sun would always appear at the end of my grandmother's garden. Was this some kind of confirmation that Jesus would land in Nino's garden? As a child, I had those kinds of thoughts, Thank God I never told anyone, or I may have very well been jokingly put away. Nino did not tell us we were living in *end times* to frighten us, but in all seriousness, to let us know that we should be ready by living a God-fearing life when Jesus returns for us.

I can remember often wandering off to myself, enjoying the rolling hillsides, the smell of pine trees, the sweat from dry earth right after a much needed rain, and eating wild strawberries, blackberries, and apples from trees laden with yellow jacket stinging bees, running from imaginary snakes, and picking dandelions and four-leaf clover plants when they were in bloom with their dainty little pink buds to make bouquets for my grandma, most of the time the bouquets were peace offerings because I knew that I had not done what she had asked me to do.

Nino never spanked us, but God knew we deserved a few whacks on our backsides from time to time. She did, however; discipline us by taking away the very thing we loved the most by making us stay inside or something even crueler in our opinion and that was to not be allowed to be by her side helping with chores which she always made a game of and somehow, very cleverly making them unbelievably fun to do.

My "wanderings" off to myself would go on until Nino would call me to supper, or to do some chore that I had conveniently forgotten or neglected to do earlier. The grown-ups would often say that I was deep in thought when I would go off on my little escapades, and indeed I was. I sometimes felt then that I alone had the burden of getting ready for Jesus for me and my brothers and sister. They were too young to have such awesome responsibilities and lofty thoughts, or so I told myself; therefore, *I* had to figure out that mystery for all of us. At the time, call it youthful folly or run-away imagination, but I honestly felt that there really wasn't anyone out there that could get my siblings ready and help them get saved for that fateful, but glorious day but me. After all, I *was* the oldest.

As stated previously, Nino never spanked us and was never harsh when she chastised any of us, especially me, because as I found out later she would lovingly tell my mother "that child is a little touched in the head", little did either of them know that even at that time I was talking to the Lord, thanking Him for all the beauty surrounding me and telling Him how much I love Him and wish I had been able to walk with Him as I someday know I will, and to walk with Jesus also when He was here on earth would have been embraced with such joy and fulfillment that the mind could not comprehend the magnitude of it all. I've often been told to be careful what we wish for. The road Jesus had to travel was far from being an easy journey. *Plus I had to get all of us ready for His return,* therefore, I would just have to put off "walking with the Father or Jesus" until they got here.

Nino, too is now in Heaven with the Lord, smiling down on me as I attempt to tell you how very special she was to us and to everyone she met, in spite of the snide remarks that some continued to make, long after my dad had moved away from what I will now and throughout this book call "Judgeville", the same little town where my dad subsequently met and married my mother, from where he went to the army to serve our country, the same little town that never allowed him to escape the stigma of being born out of wedlock, a stigma which remained an intricate part of his past which may have explained some of my dad's many weaknesses.

I often wonder if that painful stigma carried throughout his life was what eventually contributed to, if not caused my father to become an alcoholic. I am seeing an alarming pattern intertwining my life with that of my mother's, and maybe even my grandmother's life. I am especially noticing the similarities in the drinking patterns of our partners. I don't know if my grandfather on my dad's side had a drinking problem, but the way my father and my husband escaped the responsibilities of giving one hundred per cent to their families, choosing to cope with life via the bottle, is indeed uncanny.

My dad has always known the Lord and even in the depths of his alcoholic addiction, he never let go of his dependence on Jesus. Today, he no longer has the desire to take a drink, and as a matter of fact, he councils those who might turn to alcohol instead of Jesus, always letting those he talks with know that putting their trust in the Lord rather than a "bottle" is far more rewarding. He was far removed from the ominous, "drug" scene of our modern times simply due to the generation he grew up in, but his message would be the same for our youths today, if given the opportunity, and that would be to "get high on Jesus and not drugs."

My dad moved back to North Carolina from family in Tennessee (where he served in the military) a few years ago, but he now lives quite a distance from "Judgeville" and fortunately most of the pain and ostracism he experienced while growing up there has been replaced with a peace that only God can give. He had to first forgive those who were so cruel to him and his mother, then he had to accept the forgiveness that God had already given him for the bitterness he felt towards all those who had maliciously maligned his mother and the way they made him feel, which led to a lot of his doubt in his abilities to cope with life in general. My dad just had to receive this self-forgiveness from God and come to the realization that his hatred for those who hurt him was keeping him from the loving relationship he missed with his children and later, what he had and still experiences with God today after surrendering his all to the Lord.

I cannot begin to imagine what it would be like to be a child born out of wedlock, to experience the snide remarks and side-glances from people not worthy of judging anyone but doing so just the same, it would be incomprehensible from a worldly standpoint to withstand the ridicule and not retaliate in some manner, if nothing more than to tell them what hypocrites they all were. Indeed it was a cross to bear that only, as my grandmother knew and my dad has found out, can only be endured and overcome through the Love and sustaining Grace of our Lord and Savior, Jesus Christ.

Chapter Eleven: Life before the Big City

As children, before we moved to Michigan I was in the third grade, and we too lived in this small rural town in North Carolina, population approximately six hundred or so, very quaint and yet considered large for that area due to the fact that every other ten miles or so a town was named after somebody's late granddaddy. I will continue to call this little town Judgeville for the sake of privacy for those still living there or alive, elsewhere that could be inadvertently affected, either by association or embarrassment.

As stated earlier, this little town, with its' general store, post office, fire and police station all in one building, usually manned by unpaid locals, and headed by one man who wore the hat of the post master, the fire and police chief, and the mayor, was and still is *the* most beautiful town in the U.S. today. Everywhere you look, you see magnificent, majestic pine, maple, cedar and oak trees of every size and description, wild azaleas and rhododendrons, mountain laurels, hybrid ferns (then) with fronds that grew as tall as the average size ten-year-old child. The floor of the forest is carpeted with moss and pine needles year round making it an almost sensual pleasure to tread upon it.

NEVER THIS WAY AGAIN

There are mountain streams with little branches of water flowing off in one direction or another, supplying life-giving sustenance to all plants and tiny saplings in its path. These streams echo with a gurgling, calming and melodious tone that is soothing to the very soul. I am reminded of a verse found in Psalms 3:1 that states "(He is) like a tree planted by the streams of water which yields (it's fruits) in season and whose leaf does not wither."

The town even has its own unique smell. Perhaps it is all in one's mind, but the *smell* is freshness, a fragrance that penetrates and fills the air, and is experienced by everyone that either lives there or simply visits for a short while. It's a wonder that anyone would ever want to leave this ideal town once they've been there and experienced the beauty and wholesomeness the town has to offer. The majority of Judgeville's residents are from generations of families still living there with no desire to explore other parts of the world, if only for the experience of seeing how other members of society lives outside of their euphoric little world. I truly have to admire their loyalty and dedication to the preservation of a legacy that will continue throughout eternity, but that is where my admiration for this town ends. This is still due to the smug hypocrisy that remains prevalent by its residents to this day.

You will also see, snow-capped, hazy mountain tops that looks like smoke is billowing from them, and rolling hillsides covered with fragrant wild flowers, honey suckle vines, clovers and morning glories of every imaginable color and specie, as far as the eyes can see; which leaves you awestruck. Those visiting Judgeville find it difficult to truly describe it's beauty, with special emphasis paid to the foliage during the fall season when the change of colors in its entire splendor is in full array, and the snow-capped mountains, not to be out done, are giving their rendition of unbelievable beauty and awesomeness; throughout the year, but especially during the change of seasons and winter time.

The temperature in the winter gets bitterly cold, but the sheer beauty of the snow and icicles on the trees and mountaintops, almost makes one forget that in order to be comfortable while outside enjoying this beauty, one has to be dressed in multiple layers of clothing. If one does not own a full and complete wardrobe of long johns for the winter months, they are considered lower class, opposite side of the track residents.

My grandma's family fell into that less than privileged segment of society, as viewed by Judgeville's standards, but I am at a loss to understand what could have given some such a warped sense of being "better off" than others that allowed them to determine the worth of a person by how many pairs of *long drawers* they owned. Long johns aside, these frequent bouts of ignorance does not and cannot take away from the beauty that is and will forever be a part of this small town which has a legacy of unrivaled beauty and uniqueness.

Chapter Twelve: The Town of Judgeville

For the "old" money that has been in Judgeville for centuries, there are homes that depict affluent living, and there is still a couple of infamous plantation homes with too many rooms to count, with large half enclosed verandas (with half rails from the ground up) on two sides of the huge estates that get the most exposure from the sun, both with supporting, shingled roofs held up by giant stone pillars that's a notable feature of the two homes which have been preserved and designated as historical sites that boast a certain pride the residents of Judgeville *live* to tell their children about, and to encourage the retelling of their proud heritage to anyone that will listen.

The landscape, surrounding these plantation homes is something right out of "Gone with the Wind". Most spectacular are the huge Weeping Willows and the Dogwood trees laden with pink and white blossoms in springtime, with the Weeping Willows growing more imposing with each passing year. There are still many fruit, walnut and hickory nut trees, yielding as much bounty as during days of old. Corn fields now dominate most of the land on these remaining plantations where once used to be tobacco and cotton fields. The quarters that once housed the slaves are still meticulously maintained adding a sad but nostalgic air to the plantations and their rich, but infamous history.

For the not so affluent living in Judgeville, the homes are modest, but the pride of ownership is evident everywhere you look. The lawns have that manicured look, the hedges that serve as borders or boundaries instead of wooden or wire fences, are always well trimmed, and it would have been a federal offense punishable by a sentence to a lifetime of weeding servitude, if you were to ever find an imperfection in one of their flowerbeds or gardens.

My grandmother was a "domestic technician" or more commonly referred to as a maid. She worked for one of the old money families in North Carolina. They were wealthy beyond imagination, but their money did not go to their heads. They were compassionate and generous to a fault. We will call them the Bennettsons. Mr. and Mrs. Bennettson loved my grandmother and us kids too. They built the home my grandma lived in especially for her. The house was located a stone's throw from the palatial-like home of her benefactors and boss. My grandma's home was very modest in appearance, but the most beautiful house in the whole wide world to us.

The layout of Nino's house was cottage-like and very open. There was only one wall which served as a partition to separate the bedroom from the kitchen. The living and dining area was one big room divided by a larger than average, unusually designed sideboard cabinet given to her by the Bennettsons, with deep shelving and drawers to accommodate all her dishes, some of her more prized canned goods, linens, and precious treasures like the Bible and pictures she had somehow managed to hold onto of her parents, and all five of her siblings. P*icture taking* during that time was for either the rich or very rare for my grandmother's family structure. Later, there was a continuous supply of pictures of her "precious" grandchildren. This enormous, odd shaped piece of furniture also served as a partition to separate the living room from the dining area.

In my mind's eye, I see the way she cleverly hung a large mirror, the length and width of the top portion of the sideboard, which made the room look larger than it actually was, and the way she placed a beautifully designed antique brocade settee given to her by the Bennettsons below the mirror in back of the sideboard to further give the illusion of spaciousness.

In season, the house smelled of fresh flowers all the time. Nino's favorite flower was the dahlia of every color and size. She grew them in abundance anyplace she thought would be a good growing place. Needless to say, during the summer months and well into fall, her yard was like what I imagine the Garden of Eden must have looked like when it comes to comparing its beauty. She also had a penchant for growing award winning roses, huge irises and those little orange and yellow, carnation-shaped flowers that I could never remember the name of, all I know is they had a very pungent smell which I found to be very pleasant and I now know that they were Marigolds. All of these flowers in season made up the bouquets that were ever present in my grandmother's home. I try to keep fresh flowers in my home most of the time, but I must admit a lot of the times my bouquets are made up of "tacky" but very pretty artificial flowers.

The bedroom was adequately furnished with one full size iron framed bed with metal springs and a feather mattress and pillows, a small metal cot with a smaller version of the feather mattress on my grandma's bed was for my two brothers, my sister and I shared the big bed with my grandma. A couple of storage trunks for those rare and beautiful handmade quilts passed down from my grandma's mother, and one quilt passed down from her great grandmother was housed in one of those trunks. Also in the bedroom were a couple of side tables, both very valuable Gustav Stickler's, circa 1900. One table was beside the bed and the other longer table was positioned at the foot of the bed that accommodated a large vase with her flowers in season or pine branches cut to size in the winter. Both bouquets served as room fresheners at all times.

I only wish I had not been as ignorant about antiques as I later found myself to be. All of her valuable possessions were either burned up in a fire caused by a careless distant family member my dad had reluctantly allowed to stay in the house to put things in order, or they were simply given away to whoever asked for them after Nino died. I was in Michigan, too proud to ask for help to get to North Carolina to help my dad settle her estate; and alone, he was so grief stricken he did not care one way or the other who got her "things". Again, I wasn't there when Nino needed me, but I thank God the home itself wasn't totally destroyed. If one would care to go to Judgeville, they would see the house just as it was when Nino was alive. You could say, the Bennettson's allowed the structure to be refurbished and maintained as a living memorial to my grandmother.

In my mind's eye also, I can see the area used for the living-room, there was two straight back chairs with pillows on the seats that matched the upholstery on the settee, one over-stuffed green chair of no distinction in front of the large picture window, and my grandma's rocking chair that she inherited from her mom, positioned so that she also had full view of everything nature had to offer from that same large window. There were various small tables that included two very expensive, matching end tables and a cocktail table of equal value, also given to her by the Bennettsons.

To complete the décor in the living room was a very large oval area rug with large prints of purple, green and blue dahlias in its design with draperies of the same print to cover the large picture window that overlooked the entire distance of about one mile of unobstructed view from all directions; except the north side of the house, from the houses' position perched atop the hill adjacent to the Bennettsons' home. Only if she chose to close the draperies at nightfall would the panoramic view be disturbed.

I loved to look out the window at the billion stars that brilliantly cast their luster on the darkest of nights, and it was exceptionally beautiful when a full moon would cast imaginary images of angels flying among the stars. I would stare at this awesome display of nature until my grandmother would literally *make* me go to bed, or I would give up myself and go to bed because I was so sleepy that I could no longer keep my eyes open.

The Bennettsons' went to great expense to have every one of the unique, one of a kind items made or purchased for my grandmother, but that just proved how much they genuinely loved her and wanted her to be happy. I am not certain they knew the depths of her pain cause by the cruelty of judgmental people there in that nosey little town, but even if they had, I am confident they would have treated her no differently than what they did. Along with my grandmother, while she was living, and after she died, I truly thank God for the Bennettsons' and their genuine love for my grandmother and us kids.

The kitchen was an anomaly within itself. It had all the modern amenities years beyond the time period and the living conditions of the less than privileged members of society living at that time had. There was this cute little built-in cabinet which housed a double kitchen sink; one side for collecting water, the other side for washing dishes. We could pump all the water we needed instead of having to go outside to the well or spring to get our water for cooking and bathing like we had to do before the pump was installed in the kitchen. Although and despite Nino's warning of the trouble we would get into if we wasted water by playing with the pump, as curious, mischievous kids, we still had to see just how much water we could get out of the pump at once. Fortunately we had the sense not to let the water overrun onto the floor. We did not want to think of the consequences in store for us had we let this happen.

There was an unusually large oval dining table with six cane-bottomed seats and slat-back chairs that was used for both a kitchen and dining room table. We had an Ice Box (today's refrigerator) that an overweight, out of breath man would trudge, sweat oozing from every orifice, up the hill to our house every day or so to bring a big block of ice to keep our meat and other foods fresh in the ice box, but the neatest thing in the entire house was the kitchen stove that served both as a cook stove and a stove for warmth.

If I try really hard, it is almost as if I can smell the delicious baking aroma of clover-leaf yeast rolls, apple pie, rhubarb pie, peach pie, and homemade pound cake, not to mention the "pot" that consisted of any kind of meat on the menu for the day, potatoes, carrots, and onions for a stew, or a big "pot" of dried beans. At any rate these "pots" were put on in the mornings, and the stove was "banked" to allow the food to cook very slowly before Nino went to work, and would be done around noon when she came home for our afternoon meal called dinner. Our evening meal was called supper, which was always a repeat of our noon meal or something very light as not to disturb our sleep with too much on our stomachs before bedtime, if we did not have time to run off a big meal at playtime.

All of these meals were served with the homemade biscuits or cornbread that only Nino could make. The recipes were handed down from her mother and grandmother, and the techniques used to make biscuits so fluffy they would seem to be able to float in midair, or the cornbread that would melt in your mouth with such unbelievable flavor, rivaled even that of my mom's great and delicious way of cooking and baking. Nino and my mother would often share recipes, and I think bread was some of the recipes they shared.

Both Nino and my mother often shared these ageless cooking secrets with me too when I became a wife and mother, but as usual I always came up lacking when I tried to cook as they did. Maybe it was because I would always opt to eating out or buying prepared, boxed foods that kept me from spending the time needed to perfect the cooking skills handed down to me. At any rate, my children came out the loser for not being able to enjoy the matchless meals prepared for me as a child.

NEVER THIS WAY AGAIN

The stove, brand name Kitchen Comfort was a cast iron, wood burning stove sitting on four what looked like "lion paws" supporting all its giant features in total black uniqueness. The stove had four lids called "eyes" that could be lifted up with a gadget designed to open the lids which allowed us to place wood in the stove to keep the fire burning continuously. We kept the wood box beside the stove full at all times too. Although this task was indeed a chore at times, we knew the value of not allowing the wood box to become empty because then it would be a drudgery to cut and haul the enormous loads of wood necessary to fill the empty wood box again.

On top of the stove was two "warmers" that kept everything nice and warm and ready to eat before it was placed in the icebox to keep for the next day. The stove had just one oven that opened in front like our modern stoves today. Isn't it strange how one inanimate object like a wood burning, kitchen stove could leave such memories indelibly burned into one's mind? What I would give for a whiff of my grandma's cooking on that beautiful old stove today, my cooking somehow isn't quite the same; taste or smell-wise. Do you suppose it was due to that beloved old stove or is it just my desire to relive the most comfortable times of my life, I often wonder. I think most of us find that life was more comfortable when we were children, due in part to the absence of grownup responsibilities. I say this in jest, but my memories as a child are far more comforting than those of my adult life.

During our summers spent with Nino, I remember the fun we always had while she was at work, the four of us sliding down the steep hill from Nino's house on any discarded, flattened out box we could beg or sneak from her supply of boxes used for additional storage, which we used for what we called our "cars". The girls would race the boys. My sister and I always won because we knew how to win (cheat) by taking the side of the hill that was the most traveled, thereby making our side faster and less challenging to maneuver. Raymond and Rupert finally caught wind of our little deception and began to race us for the side of the hill that we had always won on. The races then became really competitive, but a lot more fun.

When we weren't racing with our homemade "race cars", we were building Indian-like tepees out of dried cornstalks left to be later picked up by Nino to put over what she called her dug out storage bin, under the back porch for sweet and white potatoes, cabbages, turnips and sometimes carrots. Our tepee was always cramped but it was large enough for the four of us to squeeze inside. There was however a definite downside to our imaginary powwows, because as we innocently called them, there were always "chicken fleas" in our little abode.

To this day I don't know what kind of cornfield insects would choose to make their meals on us, but they looked like fleas or gnats to us. After almost proudly showing who had been bitten the most, Nino would make a salve of browned flour and Vaseline and put it all over our "wounds" to make us "feel better" and not to scratch so much. I'm not clear as to what medicinal properties that concoction had, but it did stop the itching.

We also learned very quickly that our tepee was not designed to build fires in, but be as it was, we thought so. Needless to say, we caused quite a ruckus when Nino saw the flames leaping from what once was our proud structure of cornstalks and imagination. Remember we did not have access to a water hose back then to put out the fire, so we had to run up the hill repeatedly to the house and get buckets of water until the fire was out. When Nino finally calmed down enough to assess the damage to the entire section of the cornfield we were playing in and set fire to, thank God it was a very small section of the garden; we received the harshest, heartfelt verbal lashing we had ever received from her. I realize now that her reaction was in part due to the fact that she was afraid we had been injured before she actually learned that we were okay, and secondly because she had warned us about playing with matches, and as usual, our adventurous imaginations had led us to believe we could have a powwow around a big fire and smoke a peace pipe made from dried leaves and pages from an old magazine. **Big mistake**.

We also loved to go to the little country store built from roughly hewn logs and decorated midway to the ground with the prettiest fieldstones that could be found in all the surrounding area. The store, with all its goods and services, was a good mile and a half from my Nino's house. The little country store had everything the mind could possibly conceive ever needing or wanting. It was a grocery store with shelves lined with canned good both commercial and homemade, a section for cured hams and fat-back meat, flour and lard, a hardware store with plows, nails, hammers, paint, seeds and fertilizer, a pharmacy with mostly homemade remedies for colds, rheumatism or any other ailments real or imagined that one may have had, a dry good store with rolls and rolls of fabric for clothing or anything else one would care to use the cloth for, and a mill for grinding corn into cornmeal, all under one overstocked roof.

My grandmother would send us to the store with a quarter, which was big bucks back then, and we would get a nickel's worth of flour or cornmeal, a dime's worth of salt pork or fat back meat, a pound of lard, a nickel's worth of sugar and some dried beans or peas, all for that *one* quarter. Believe it or not, these items would last for at least a couple of weeks, and we had plenty to eat for that period of time just from those purchased staples added with the fresh or canned foods Nino always had on hand in large supply. As I think back to our adventures to and from the store, the echo of Nino's reminders each time we went to the store brings an unbearable sadness to me now because we, as "colored" people could only shop in certain areas of the store and we always had to go to the side of the store to a window designated for "coloreds" to buy our favorite ice cream or soda pop, but we still anxiously looked forward to the next two weeks when we would again have to do battle with our imaginary foes to and from the store.

We especially loved the hand churned strawberry ice cream and the ice cold grape or orange sodas that we could get as special treats if we were especially good, this meant by not getting into our usual bouts of fighting and arguing with one another about what turned out to be trivial, but very big to us at the time or so we told ourselves. There were other mischievous acts we were known for that guaranteed we wouldn't get rewarded for like playing with matches or "stealing" cookies or muffins and then blaming another sibling for it Ray usually was the culprit, but he would always say that one of us had stolen the sweet treat to keep himself out of trouble. *Nino hated lying.*

We were also rewarded for doing the simple chores assigned to us like washing the dishes, sweeping the floors or filling the wood-box beside the stove for cooking while my grandma was at work. As stated earlier, there was a couple of drawbacks to going to that store, one being in the late 1940's and early 50's, people of color weren't allowed to go inside to the restaurants but were allowed to purchase items from the restaurant or deli at a window specifically designed to accommodate its non-white patrons. We did not know anything was wrong with this practice until we permanently moved to Michigan a few years later. We sadly felt then that it was an accepted part of our lives.

Thank God for our innocence and the kindness of the Bennettson's. The other more disturbing drawback, at least to us was this one particular bridge that we had to cross over which was probably originally designed for a horse and buggy but would allow a car to narrowly cross over it. Under this bridge was a small, almost dried up creek with "creepy, crawly" things in it which made all our imaginations run wild at the thought of the monsters" that lived under the water of that creek. Adjacent to the creek on either side was an over-grown, swamp-like, snake infested area that was a part of the bridge that we could not escape passing by if we wanted to get to our destination, the store.

In our over active imaginations, we would even see snakes disguised in the stems of the enormous cattail plants that were famous for the swamps in our part of North Carolina. Isn't it strange how we never thought about snakes or any of the other dangers lurking in the bushes or under rocks while we were playing at any place other than that bridge while at my grandma's? We did not think that snakes slithered from place to place as a normal part of nature; that idea or reality simply was not a part of our rationale.

Going to the store was a true act of bravery on our parts no matter how much we loved and lived for the treats we'd get from there, we were deathly afraid of the snakes that seem to live in the swamp and even in the half dead, enormously large willow tree, frighteningly looming on the left side of the creek with gnarled-limbs hovering over the bridge. Snakes were *everywhere*. I cannot count the times Nino had to come and get us because we were frozen in fear and would not cross the bridge until she came to get us because we had either seen a snake or thought we heard one while enroute to the store or coming back on our way home.

Most of the snakes were non-poisonous like Garter or King snakes, but there had on occasion been seen a Blue Racer or an occasional Water Moccasin, both very poisonous, which added to the paralyzing fear we had of the creepy crawlers. The only other time we had even heard of a Blue Racer snake was when an acquaintance (we think he was "sweet" on Nino) of my grandma's was trying to scare us kids by telling us the Blue Racer was at the old saw mill, where the snake would catch a kid and put his head in their nose and beat them (with his tail) while the snake was suffocating its victim.. The trips to the saw mill to gather wood with our grandma was never quite the same after that.

Again I ask, isn't it strange how we never gave thought to snakes when we were playing, maybe in our minds, where we played was far, far away from that bridge and the creepy swamp, (and the saw mill) filled with snakes. At any rate, poisonous or not, we hated snakes and wanted no part of them.

NEVER THIS WAY AGAIN

I can see Nino now, a slender, middle aged woman with medium brown complexion, bobbed cut hair graying ever so slightly, and being a tad taller version of my mother in every way appearance wise, with her hands on her hips, shaking her head in disbelief that we could be genuinely scared out of our pants at the mere thought of snakes, not believing for a moment that we had actually seen a snake due to the fact that we had used that worn out story many times to get away with our lingering in play rather than just returning home as we should have, not to mention the tall tales regarding the several snakes we had told her were actually *chasing* us, which did nothing for our integrity with her, which in turn had to be secretly, very humorous to her, but her outward expression was that of disbelief and knowing we had told her a series of falsehoods again.

Most times, if the truth were told, there wasn't really a snake anywhere; the "snakes" were just slithering around in our vivid, overactive imaginations and if indeed there were snakes, they were probably more afraid of us than we were of them at least this is what Nino often told us.

In all our time with Nino, we had only truthfully seen about five or six snakes, which slithered away as fast as they could to get away from us. She would repeatedly assure us that the snakes were more afraid of us than we were of them. I don't know about my sister and brothers, but it was not humanly (or animally-my word) possible for anyone or anything to be more "pee in your pants", afraid of snakes than I was, and I suppose to be very honest with you that if I had really seen a snake while freely roaming about in my times of "reflection", I would have stayed a lot closer to the house.

During the winter months that we stayed with my grandmother, no matter how cold it got outside, it was always warm and cozy inside because we kept plenty wood in the wood box and just outside the kitchen door to "bank" the fire at night so that a fire was going at all times during those *cold* months. It makes me sad even now when I think back to the time when my grandmother would have to go to the woods and tote wood back to her house when we weren't there to help her, but after a while, when she was unable to do this chore for herself because of her "rheumatism", the Bennettsons' arranged for someone to bring her wood whenever she needed it. All she had to do was let them know that she was getting low on wood, and before she got the request out of her mouth, or so it seemed, a truck would be backing up to her kitchen door with a large load of wood, enough to last her for a month or so.

The only other negative thing I remember about being at my grandma's, other than the snakes, was that the toilet or bathroom was at the back of the house with no way to heat it during the winter months. This was before portable space heaters. Although, the bathroom *was attached* to the house, I don't have to tell you that we all learned to "hold" whatever nature's call was until the very last moment, then with great reluctance we would brace ourselves for what we dreaded would be the inevitable "frostbite" on our hinnies during that trek to the toilet during those dreaded winter months. If my description of the unheated bathroom and what it took to go there when it was frostbiting cold seems like an exaggeration, *it is not.* I thank God those days are now over. That bathroom, or privies as they were called, reminded me of the times we had to go out to the back forty in Michigan before our bathroom was upgraded to the twentieth century.

If you're fortunate enough or too young to remember the *wonderful* days of heat-free bathrooms, you would be surprised to know how long one could actually hold back the urges of nature, when it was hard to decide whether you'd rather risk the indignity of wetting your pants or suffer a worse fate by going into a room likened unto a deep freezer with the hope that you would not freeze your buns off would astound you.

I *must* candidly confess, for the two winters we lived with my grandmother, I had that decision to go or not to go, to make more times than I care to remember, and there was a lot of times I waited just a little too long. Because of embarrassment, I won't tell you what personally happened to me, but it doesn't take a rocket scientist to know what really happened each and every time I played wait and see with my bladder.

Finally, a winter after we returned to Michigan, the Bennettsons' bought a kerosene heater to put in the bathroom to keep it warm for Nino. This was not an oversight on their part; Nino just had never complained that it was too cold in the bathroom or to make them aware of the fact that no heat in the bathroom bothered Nino. This silence on Nino's part made her have to endure the cold a lot longer than she had to. That is why the Bennettsons' had not gotten around to correcting the situation any sooner than they did. Eventually, three years to be exact, before Nino died, the Bennettson's ran electrical wiring into the bathroom, installed an oversized bathtub in addition to the shower already there for her convenience *and* specifically for her to "soak" her aching joints caused by her "rheumatism". This added luxury made Nino feel like she had already "died and gone to heaven" before she actually got there. It is really funny how the *simplest* thing or conveniences can bring such happiness and contentment in the simplest of ways.

It was hard to determine which room Nino loved the most because she was so very grateful for her *entire* beautiful home. Although she never held a lot of regard for material "things", I honestly believe that through the generosity and genuine caring the Bennettsons' showed her, she finally felt that her sins had been forgiven, and her past was just that, her past. Anyway, that is the impression I always got when talking with her when I inquired regarding her well-being whether there with her or by way of letter that she always had someone from her church write for her.

NEVER THIS WAY AGAIN

Although Nino only went to the sixth grade, she was more than capable of writing letters herself, but after the rheumatism crippled her hands, she had to ask someone to write letters and any other correspondence that required writing. Her desire to keep in touch with us when we were away, made her put her pride about asking someone to do something as private as writing a letter for her, was put on the back burner. The letters shared from all of us after we got grown, kept us connected although we were more than nine hundred miles apart. This also kept Nino and my dad current with all that was going on with us, like if there were any new additions to our families, or if some of us had new love interests, and if so, who, or when were either of us coming to visit, etc.

Chapter Thirteen: The Big City

As stated earlier, we lived in Judgeville until I was in the third grade, then we moved to Michigan where I completed high school and much later finished college, married twice and had two children from each marriage.

The "big city" was such a drastic change from the "we know everybody's business" town we had come from, that even as a child it took some getting used to. We lived in the city with all the same nosey, gossiping neighbors (possibly more) that we grew up with in Judgeville, and yes there were also good, God fearing neighbors in the big city too, and the people dynamics were the same as everywhere else in the world, except there was an unwelcome closeness of houses that took some getting used to, if ever.

The neighbors were all over the place, hanging over each other's fences gossiping about the very same person they had just finished talking with, or running out of each other's houses borrowing sugar, coffee, flour, eggs or whatever was needed instead of just going to the store to buy those "borrowed" items. Maybe this odd behavior was due to a lack of money until the next payday, or worse yet, an unconventional way of bonding with one another.

You figure it out. I must be very careful not to minimize their need to borrow from one another because I had not experienced poverty yet.

The children often screamed for attention, doing whatever their little minds could conceive that would get attention to no avail while their mothers were either on the phone gossiping or outside hanging over a fence, or sitting on the porch or porch steps, *gossiping*. It simply *did not* matter. It seemed that their days were equally divided between haphazardly running their households and *gossiping*. Rue avoided this interaction with her neighbors like a plague, stating that gossip was like idleness, firmly believing both were from the "devil's workshop".

I personally found their topics of conversation about one another to be very amusing, and would often be caught by my mother on the many occasions when I would be secretly, or so I thought, eavesdropping. I would always get a tongue lashing not to be forgotten for my obvious enjoyment to being privy to this *sin*. Rue had little, if any tolerance for, or patience with my *weakness* for secretly enjoying with great amusement their gossiping. My mother was always admonishing me for fear that I might turn out just like them because of the obvious pleasure derived from witnessing their idleness. When all her warnings to stop taking pleasure in hearing what the neighbors were gossiping about failed, the threat of the infamous *rod* for this childish but *wrong* indulgence was my next option if I continued with something Rue considered to be sinful.

Whether we wanted to know or not, no one was really given a choice. We had only to pass by a neighbors' home to know what was for dinner because the aromas of cooking was everywhere especially that of cabbage cooking every day in one house or another. There was always smells of fried chicken or fish no matter what day of the week it was. These were not pleasant cooking odors or comforting aromas as experienced with my mother and grandma's cooking. They were almost offensive odors due to the possibility that the cooking oils were used over and over again making the smell of fried foods, rank.

Usually, and somehow traditionally, Fridays always seemed to be fish day in North Carolina, but not on our block except for one day in particular. We always knew it was Wednesday because, you guessed it, that was spaghetti day for everyone, no exceptions. There was no central air conditioning back then, especially in our neighborhood, therefore doors and windows were wide open always except in the dead of winter allowing all the smells of cooking good or bad, mostly bad, to escape freely.

Equally pungent, was the smell of garbage in some overturned garbage can in the alley behind many homes where stray dogs and cats fed regularly from the discarded food that was carelessly thrown out by someone not wanting the task of taking out the garbage in the first place? Needless to say, there was an over population of rats and mice just waiting to invite themselves into somebody's house the first chance they found available, especially into the homes that did not have a "mouser" better known as a cat.

We did not know it at the time but thankfully we would eventually get back to our "roots" much sooner than we thought after my mother's second husband died, and although the circumstances were not the best to begin with, it was a welcomed and grateful change. Anything, in our opinion, would be better than living in a place that we felt was totally foreign to the life we had become accustomed to while living in Judgeville prior to our move to the city. That move back to what we called "normal" for us, would eventually shape all our futures.

We often hear that children are very resilient and can adapt to change much quicker than adults, while this may be true in some instances, I did not find this statement to be true at all. I missed the openness of the country around me, the abundance of trees, the fields of vegetation and wild flowers with fragrances so pungent, I can almost smell them now, the sounds of crickets, birds, and owls at night and fresh *smog-free* air. I did not like that the houses were so close that we could reach out any window and shake our neighbor's hand, nor did I like the smell of exhaust fumes from the over population of cars desperately needing repairs of one degree or another.

I assure any of you city dwellers that this statement about the closeness of the houses may be an exaggeration on my part, but as a child it sure seemed that way to me at the time. I apologize if this statement is offensive to anyone. I suppose when one is accustomed to roaming the hillsides and seeing vast spaces with no houses for miles, the shock of city life and the overly familiarity of neighbors kind of makes everything in this new environment seem cramped and suffocating in comparison.

I too, now live in the city, but the home I purchased is on a doublewide lot, and even if I wanted to, I cannot hear the neighbors unless we're both outside and choose to talk with one another. Perhaps, this is a far stretch from what and how God intended neighbors to feel toward one another, but at the same time, I do not believe that our Heavenly Father wanted us to be in one another's business at any time, unless invited. I still, however pray for a balance in this situation and the way I feel about neighbors in general, because I am reminded of Gods' commandment that "we should love our neighbors as ourselves" Lev. 19:18.

I feel a deep sense of shame for not always adhering to the literal word of God regarding my neighbors. As a Christian, I am in daily conflict regarding some neighbors that make it almost impossible to love them. I guess those neighbors are like the thorn in the side Apostle Paul referred to. Although his "thorn in the side" wasn't a neighbor, whatever it was Paul had to simply resign himself to the fact that God's Grace was sufficient for him. I too, must take this same position. 2 Cor. 12:7.

When we moved to Michigan, it meant leaving my grandmother, which was just as traumatic for me as it was when she died some fifteen or so years later. The only other time I can remember crying more or as much was when my mother, and later my firstborn died in an auto accident along with by youngest brother Rupert. I did not have my mom or my grandmother to lean on for strength when my son and my baby brother died, but their passing only affirmed the lessons I learned by example from Rue and Nino. I finally realized the strength and moral fortitude that was an intricate part of their personalities and strength to endure the tragedies forever present in their lives was given to them only by God, and thankfully to me as well.

My son was fourteen and my brother was age twenty-five when they died. They were returning from a pancake social where my brother worked at the local junior high school as a custodian and had taken my son along to help, when a drunk driver causing the accident that killed them both, ran them off the road. For reasons I do not understand (like today) to this day, no one was ever charged with causing their death, it was almost as if their deaths were of little, or of any significance to authorities. The pain of their loss was so overpowering that I did not have the strength to pursue the criminal aspects involved with pushing the legal system to investigate their deaths more vigorously, so I guess you could say that I simply let their killers get away with murder. At any rate, this is how I felt for a long time; that is until God allowed me to see that He would and did take care of the situation for me. *Anything hidden in the dark will always come to light.*

Looking back at my not acting to do what I should have done to address this painfully paralyzing time in my life also brings me back to the time when my grandma died from a diabetic coma that she never came out of, I had just lost a job that meant everything to me and my husband had also recently passed from causes brought on by him and his poor, selfish decisions. Too much for me to digest in such an unusually short time

Conditions were not the best for me financially. Regrettably, I missed the chance to say goodbye to Nino because I did not have the financial means to get back to North Carolina. I learned after the shock of losing her subsided that my not getting there could have been avoided if I had not allowed my "stupid" pride to prevent me from asking for help to get to her before she died, but because of this sinful *pride*, I lost one of the most precious, last moment interactions we could have ever experienced in either of our lives.

Had I known then what I know now, I would have put my sinful pride aside and gone to the American Red Cross, my church, or some other agency that would have helped me financially to be with her during her last moments here on earth, to offer her the same love and comfort she had so unselfishly and generously given to me and my siblings throughout our entire lives with her. I pray that she forgave me before she left here, and then again, knowing her, there wasn't an unforgiving bone in her body, and I thank God every day for this revelation, because without this word from Him, I would still be laden with enormous guilt for not being there when I feel she needed *me* the most.

I thank God every day for Blessing me to have had a mother and a grandmother like I was privileged to have had in both of them. I look back at their lives and the many obstacles they had to overcome coupled with the simplicity, but powerful measures of faith they both had in God, which outwardly made otherwise difficult situations seem minor to them. Compared to witnessing firsthand everything they both endured and still remained faithful in their walk with Christ was amazing, then to even have to think about going through life and its circumstances without having the love and mercy of our Father God, makes me sad. But when we freely accept the Grace he gives us as they did, to be victorious over life's many problems, it is indeed worthy of Praise to our Lord and Savior Jesus Christ for giving us the ability to overcome life's little "hard knocks" no matter how difficult we perceive them to be while in the deepest throes of our trials and valleys.

Sometimes in our worldly way of thinking, it escapes our understanding that all things could and would be so much simpler if only we would allow God to have His Way in our lives. Simply stated, *our lives would be far less complicated.* We would hurt less emotionally, we would know without doubt that our happiness is not dependent on mans' whims, but on the very Word of our Lord and Savior Jesus Christ. Unfortunately this is something I am only beginning to understand fully.

I truly count it a blessing to know that God loves *me* enough to be concerned about my every care. I personally do not understand most of the decisions He has made regarding my life, but I can honestly say that I thank Him because there is nothing done under the sun that God does not have total and complete control over. This trust goes doubly when it comes to accepting His love and intervention with the situation I am dealing with while trying to understand why my children seem less than loving and compassionate towards me. I only want Him to make it better so that I can stop hurting. I also know that this may take time; time that my patience feels is an eternity, but having to realize again that His time is measured totally and differently than mine makes waiting for the desired change a little easier.

Chapter Fourteen: Retrospections

Now that the reality of death is imminent, I often wonder what contributions have I made for and to my children and their children with reference to how or what we all should do to show appreciation for our parents? From where I sit, it doesn't appear that I've provided much substance to their perception as to how "older" people are to be regarded and appreciated for the wisdom that they have gained and are endowed with to have helped them realize the God inspired insights that only come with age.

I make this observation based on everyday interactions or the lack of those that I have with my own children. Don't misunderstand my premise; I am again fully aware mentally, but not always, emotionally that our sole responsibility as parents is to raise our kids to be productive, law-abiding grown-up adults that will in turn raise their offspring's to be the same. But knowing this, especially when our hearts are breaking because of the insensitive actions of our children, is not always the most comfortable place in life to be in at *any* given time or age.

Genesis 2:24 says "Therefore shall a man leave his father and mother, and shall cleave unto his wife: and they shall become one flesh." The Lord plainly, without room for confusion lets us know the role we have as parents when our children become adults. I am going to paraphrase this mandate from God by saying that the Lord wants us to love our children, to be there for them in an advisory capacity, *when asked*, but to mind our own business and let them live their lives as we expected our parents to let us live our lives. *Amen.*

Now for a discussion that is unfortunately unpopular to most adult children today. "Older" parents *are not* a burden. I cannot speak for all aged or aging parents, nor would I assume that all adult children are "selfish little brats", but I will say for those parents that have felt the sting of rejection, it is not a place that anyone with "feelings" that can still count to ten would want to visit. Just imagine, for the sake of argument that your child or children came to you one day, out of the blue, and told you that they could no longer devote the time they had previously given you because their other obligations dictated otherwise, what would you really think or feel?

I know out of a sense of pride, and an unselfish love for your adult children, you would say that you totally understood this new development in both your lives, but if you were to be perfectly honest with yourself, you would momentarily feel rejected and abandoned just like everyone else that is not ashamed to admit this unpleasant fact. Maybe abandonment and rejection is too strong of a description for this emotion and perhaps not even shared to the same degree by all, but the pain of not being needed anymore would be there just the same.

Do we become more sensitive as we age, with reference to the magnitude of emotions we feel, or are our perception of how we're being treated by our children, just a matter of being *oversensitive*? You tell me. Is it just a matter of how we perceive this uncomfortable condition, or is it really a condition that is valid, but not accepted by anyone that hasn't experienced this unfortunate situation yet? I say yet because we will, at one time or another as parents feel the sting of rejection whether in a big way or in such a way that the symptoms are so mild that we can or tend to overlook the entire phenomenon.

Is it possible to love our children too much? Can we so blindly put so much of ourselves into raising our children that we lose the ability to recognize that we were once someone other than a mother or father? It is very obvious from the experiences with my mother and grandmother that being a mother is sometimes a thankless job, but at the same time, I do not think any mother that accepts the job of motherhood, would have it any other way.

I personally did not appreciate the sacrifices that were made on my behalf by the two women I loved more than anything in this world; equally with the love I have for my children. However, I was not able to show this love while they both were alive in the manner they both deserved to see. It was a *shameful* disservice on my part to both of them. That shame remains to this day. Unfortunately there are still mothers out there needing only to be acknowledged by *those* they have sacrificed the most for throughout their sometimes, ungrateful, unappreciative lives, but these mothers (and grandmothers) are having to resign themselves to the fact that their "precious darlings" are clueless to their need to just be acknowledged and respected for the viable human beings they still are.

You have probably noticed by now that not a lot of references have been made regarding the significant males in the lives of my mother, grandmother or me. Could it be because although my mother and I were married more than once, we both had the tendency to find husbands that were less than "strong" role models? I don't know if this was a conscious act of selection or if it was simply something in our makeup that just naturally attracted men that did not mind the woman being the dominant mate in the relationship.

Whatever the dynamics in place during the selection process were, it truly left a lot to be desired when it came to portraying a God anointed family unit that was headed by a husband and father, which by Christian and societal standards would have been the model for a functional family unit the way the family should be structured, and ultimately the way the Lord designed it to be.

Chapter Fifteen: Less than Perfect Parenting

This brings me to the lack of parenting provided by the father of my children. Neither father expressed any desire to do more than "provide" for his children and I guess by today's standards, where in some instances the state is the sole provider for far too many children "providing" for one's children is better than abandoning responsibility for them all together. Looking again at today's standards, the role each of my husbands played as fathers thankfully was the lesser of the two evils. They provided financially for our children but left that crucial element of emotional support out of the equation. There however *must* be a balance. Yes, children must be provided for but having the bonding, love and nurturing from *both* parents is *equally* and *critically* important.

This too, might explain why there was and still is very little respect shown for their fathers, as the respect for fathers in Christ centered homes are shown. Our Father God gave very explicit instructions as to the role of both father and mother. Simply stated, "Train up a child in the way he should go, and when he is old he will not depart from it". Proverbs 22:6. Another of the many pearls of wisdom on childrearing found in God's instructions for us as parents, but when we fall short of adhering to God's instructions as parents, there is little need to wonder why our children grow up to be less than overly respectful and involved with us.

I did not condone the children's lack of respect for their fathers, but I did not vigorously chasten them for their attitudes" toward them either. I take full responsibility for my less than Christian-like response to the situation, but what I perceived to be the role of my husband and the father to our children was far from being demonstrated in our everyday familial interactions.

I guess you could say, that I was in a form of rebellion, desiring what I felt should have been but ideally wasn't. The model of the "ideal family" left a lot to be desired compared to normal and accepted standards than what it really was for us. Simply stated, it was nothing like God said it should be and after a while, there was no effort on either of our part to make the situation or the dysfunctional dynamics in our family any better. In other words our concept of how a family should function was in direct conflict with God's design and plans for any family. To put it mildly another way, if that is possible, we were in direct *disobedience* to the instructions set forth in God's Word pertaining to His instructions for a functional, God favored family unit.

I never mentioned the fact that despite my upbringing, I chose both husbands with identical qualities. Both were unbelievably good looking, built like champion body builders, and unknowingly at the time, they both allowed me to be the "boss" stating that "when I was happy, everyone else was happy". Little did I know then, but sadly discovered later, in both marriages, that we were blatantly, unequally yoked. 2 Corinthians 6:14 states, "Be ye not unequally yoked with unbelievers: for what fellowship hath righteousness with unrighteousness? And what communion hath light with darkness?"

Neither husbands went to church, but had no objection to me taking the children to church. They would make sure we had money to pay our tithes and offerings when I ran short of money, but to get either of them into a church building was like pulling hen's teeth. Yes, they both believed in God but neither had a personal relationship with Him until they realized they would have to stand before Him in a very short time. I could be wrong, but I truly feel that both husbands either felt or knew that death was near for both of them. Knowing they each had time to "get their houses in order" by making peace with God, is comforting to a great extent. Again, thanks are for God's mercy and grace which made it possible for both of them to make peace with God before they died. My only regret is that our children did not see this transformation in them until they were literally on their dying beds.

Here we go again with that "hindsight" thing. I'm asking myself could this, my example of hastily, although not feeling this way at the time, the choosing of my mates as having no real desire to lead by example be the reason for my children's self-absorption? And if by example, did I unwittingly plant the seed of selfishness and of not having a problem with detachment in them take on a life of its own? I pray this is not the case, because the realization that I am somehow responsible for my adult children's uncaring attitudes and behavior makes the suffering I "feel" I'm going through even harder to bear.

Is there truth in the old adage that states," The fruit does not fall too far from the tree"? If that adage has an ounce of truth to it, may God have mercy on some of us, especially me because if we must place blame on someone or something, it can only be ourselves. Doesn't it make us feel better knowing that others have made the same dumb mistakes we've made in our attempts to be that parent that knew everything or thought we did? I only say this to us parents that can admit that we were less than perfect when it came to raising our children, and not to those parents that are still perfect, raising perfect kids. If there is such a person, living on this planet today, please email me, cbp@ notaperfectparent.com and share with me and eventually the world *your* secret.

Chapter Sixteen: Reflections

"Guilt", such an ugly word, has a way of making us either take an honest "inventory" of ourselves, or imitate the ostrich and hide our head in the sand and pretend that everything that is happening or has happened, and will happen in the future is totally out of our control, and would not be happening if it weren't someone else's fault. We tend to forget that our Father God made us all with a mind to be able to make decisions, whether informed or uninformed, we are blessed with that capability. It is therefore up to us, individually, to decide what path we will take in this life. And whatever decisions we make, we must be adult enough to accept the consequences, good or not so good when life turns out differently than how we planned it.

I chose the only path I knew, and that was and still is, motherhood. I won't say that I wasted money getting a four-year college degree, and the time spent in graduate studies, nor will I say that the six (I took a couple of years off) years out of my life pursuing that degree was a waste of time either, but my true calling was motherhood and I make no apologies for it. Looking back, I truly wonder if I had been able to devote all my time to a career, would my life have been fuller. I will never know because I *chose* motherhood instead, a job that is not a part time position no matter how multi-faceted or super task oriented we think we are. There are many mothers out there that is balancing that fine line between motherhood and career and doing an excellent job, but I did not have what it took to do both and I am comfortable with the fact now that I chose motherhood over career.

Although all my children are grown and leading productive lives by the worlds' standards, there's something amiss. What happened to "I love you Mom" or "how do you feel today, Mom"? Have becoming adults with busy lives of their own, made them forget that it's a simple show of compassion that doesn't take much from their busy schedules to just pick up the phone and call an aging parent. Does this simple act of kindness escape their realm of understanding? I sincerely hope not, because that finger of guilt is pointing, accusingly straight at me again saying "it's how *you* raised them". It's too bad we can't blame God for how He made us, because then we could make excuses for the dumb mistakes we make over and over again, without giving a second thought to the error of our ways, or to make any attempt to correct our short comings.

I have often wondered why we never really understand the magnitude of Gods' love for us. Is there some innate insensitivity, regarding anything other than ourselves that make us unaware of the sacrifices those before us have made, or are we just simply creatures of the "me", "mine", and "my" mentality? I know that this is and never was God's purpose for us. His purpose for us is evident in His creation of the first family, Adam and Eve. It was only after "self" became operative causing them to sin that the love God intended eternally for us in a sinless paradise, was challenged by the enemy Lucifer causing us to become the selfish, willfully sinful people we oft time tend to be even to this day.

I have also tried, unsuccessfully I might add to understand how we so easily forget what God clearly stated again when He instructed us to "leave our parents and cleave to our mates". Mark 10:7 states, "For this reason a man shall leave his father and mother and be joined to his wife." While I trust and believe in the infallible Word of God, I personally have a problem with how literal we take this statement, and this is evidenced by the overcrowded nursing homes that are in our midst today, where some of the elderly residents or patients are for the most part have been forgotten by their children in exchange for the "life" that they, the adult children are "entitled" to live predicated by the argument that "they, the parents have lived their lives, now it is time for *me* to live mine" It is the mentality which very often allows the adult child to conveniently forget that the bulk of the life "lived" by their parents were devoted to getting them to where and what they are today.

Before I go any further, let me just say that all I've said so far is not a blanket indictment or is it relevant to all children because there are some wonderful, caring, and genuinely compassionate adult "children" that have learned to balance their schedules to accommodate an occasional, *meaningful* visit with their parents. They have not forgotten the need of their parents to "feel" they are still important to them. I guess this does not become an issue for any of us until it smacks us open-handed, with force, on the face, making us realize that we as parents do not hold the prominent, exclusive place in our children's lives as we once did before they became adults.

I do not believe there's a parent alive today that would want their children to remain dependent on them. If anything, most parents are "pushing" their "precious little darlings" out of the nest as quickly as possible. Isn't that why some of us go without new clothes, always second time around garments and shoes, drive a car held together by used parts, retreads, clothes hangers and crazy glue, and to only visit the beauty or barber shop via television or magazines, just to make certain that our precious little ones are equipped with everything that is needed to survive in this great big, unforgiving "mean old world"?

I will not embarrass my remaining children by divulging which one has caused me the most emotional pain, but let's just say, "It was and still is the squeaky wheel that got and still gets the oil". I would be utterly amazed if there wasn't one such child in every family. These little "darlings" are the ones that tell you that they will never leave you, that they are going to buy you a great big house when they get "growd up", and that they will *never* marry because they want to "live" with you forever. I'm smiling as I write this because it was so cute and heartwarming to hear my child say these things, and at the time, nothing could have convinced this child at age three that this wasn't exactly how life was going to be, just them and their mom. How quickly they change.

I can't help but to be saddened when I think of the pain and grief we daily cause our Heavenly Father, when we deliberately sin against Him by not caring for our elderly parents, and just as importantly our elderly brothers and sisters in Christ. How hard can it be to just pick up a telephone or our cell phones and call our parents and other older people to see if they're okay, if they need anything, or simply to say hello, how are you doing, and I love you? But, it is only after I have become an "aging" parent myself can I heartbreakingly see the pain this condition causes all parents that feel their children have abandoned them all together. *Whether it is real or perceived,* in most instances the phenomenon is real.

As I stated earlier, God in His infinite wisdom and mercy has given us His promise that He will be with us when everyone else has forsaken us. Hebrews 13:5 states the Lord promise where it says "He will never leave us or forsake us." We must always draw strength from this irrefutable truth in spite of how we as mere human beings may *feel.*

We often tend to mistakenly put our trust in man when we know fully that the outcome will be fruitless, but it seems to always be the option we choose. It is unfortunately, our nature to depend on those people or things that we view as tangible to provide the comfort and support we need when we're hurting instead of depending on the true source of our deliverance. The one true Source that will deliver us from *all* the ills we are experiencing, the one and only Source that is the total dependence on God and His Word.

Chapter Seventeen: The Other Side

I choose not to point a finger by naming anyone, or giving specifics about incidents that have occurred outside of my own personal experiences that brought about this outpouring of emotions, but I will *admonish* all those that neglect the person called mom or dad. I do not make these assertions based on every adult child's behavior, only for those that may look back one day and have to pray God's forgiveness for your unintentional or unconscious acts of disrespect or for your inconsiderate and selfish behavior towards your parents after they're gone as I have sadly had to do.

At the risk of sounding redundant again, I'm not asking nor do I expect any adult "child" to put their lives on hold until their parents are dancing around in Glory, but I will never tire of entreating each of you to acknowledge and respect those that got you to where you are today as more than just, if not a burden, an inconvenience that gets in the way of how you would like to be "living" your life free from the unwanted responsibilities of caring for or "catering" to the whims or demands of an aging parent.

Now, let's address the other side of the parenthood spectrum. Every man that plants a "seed" and every woman that conceives and gives birth does not necessarily have what it takes to be an effective and loving parent. To the unfortunate "children" conceived in this haphazard way, it would be pretty hard to expect them to be the "devoted child" to people whose responsibility ended when either conception or the birth took place.

Unfortunately, statistics bear out the fact that the "feel good", "don't want or need the baggage" attitude is prevalent today and is insidiously becoming an accepted norm. Even so, God still expects us to honor and love those responsible for us being here. By any of us being here, who knows or can foresee what great plans the Lord has made for our lives. Only God knows our destinies, because as stated in Jeremiah 1:5 "While yet in the womb, He knew us." Isn't this an awesome revelation? *God does not make mistakes.*

Again, without pointing a finger or being "judgmental", I think of all the babies that will have to grow up never knowing what it feels like to have nurturing and selfless parents that planned their arrival, and upon that arrival, showered them with the love that can only be compared in a very small measure to Gods' love for us. When a child does not experience this bonding based on love, is in some instances, criminal.

Unfair as it may seem, these children are the lucky ones because at least they had the chance to come into the world whereas in comparison there are countless number of babies that ended up in the abortionist's mill. This too (abortion) has grievously become an accepted norm by a lot of Right to Choose advocates out there. May God have Mercy on *all* of us?

I made reference earlier to the fact that God has a way of letting us know whom we can depend on, and that reference ties into the observations made regarding the lack of parenting demonstrated by "baby makers" exclusively. This takes me back to the fact that I have not had the privilege of truly knowing or bonding with my earthly father, not because there wasn't an unfulfilled desire to know him, but out of some crazy sense he had of "I'll show them" attitude, meaning everyone he felt was not compassionate towards him and the conditions he was born into nor had any control of made his ineptness and the shirking from his fatherly duties seem acceptable to him.

While I don't understand his standoffish attitude towards us, his biological children, especially since he did not have a relationship with his father, one would think that this fact alone would have made him want to be a devoted, ever present father for us. At any rate, this omission on his part to fatherhood is something he will have to ultimately settle with God.

My dad still has difficulties relating to me on a more personal level, but he has learned to reluctantly share his feeling of love for me even at this late juncture in both our lives. I have to wonder if by the abandonment by his father, did this void in his life; make him incapable of showing his love for us children in a more demonstrative way? Again, only God can answer this question for me because my dad has no desire to acknowledge the pain he has caused all of his children by being so very distant. He tells me he loves me, but I have to wonder again how much of this is genuine, and how much of his claim of love for me is what he feels I need to hear? God knows.

God has been there for me so completely, that the pain of not having a father that I felt truly loved me, has finally been accepted after many years of wondering what I did to make my dad so very irresponsible and uncaring, but despite his obvious rejection of me and my siblings, when they were alive, just makes me pray harder for him, and love him unconditionally, as I know the Lord loves me and commands that I love and honor my dad. I won't attempt to analyze our relationship, simply because it is not my place, but I will venture to say that something, someone, or sometime in his life, he was injured to the extent that it would explain the difficulty he has when it comes to being totally open with me, or my brothers and sister when they were alive.

You know, now that I think back there was never a discussion between my brothers and sister regarding our father, even after we all reached adulthood. Do you suppose it was because like me they had accepted the fact that our dad was responsible for making us and that is where the connection ended? You would think there would have been the normal curiosity most kids have about an absent parent, but there strangely wasn't, and similar to my dad's reluctance to discuss his dad with my grandmother, maybe there were questions that simply did not get asked.

Chapter Eighteen: Irreplaceable Losses

  I genuinely love my younger brothers and sisters from my mother's second marriage, very much but there wasn't the closeness shared among us that was present with us four older children. There is a ten year difference between me the oldest of my mother's children by her first marriage to the oldest child by her marriage to my step-dad. My sister, Rosalind died first from a brain aneurysm caused by what some called an act of violence if so, no one was ever prosecuted. At the age of twenty-five she left four minor children that my mother raised along with her already established, mighty brood.

  Then Rupert died next at age twenty-five in an auto accident that not only took him in death, but my fourteen-year-old son as well. His untimely death also left four very young children just as my sister had but his wife Dana, who married again shortly after Rupert's death to get help with bringing their children up. She was only twenty-three when my brother died and desperately needed the help. We understood why she married so quickly after Rupert's death, less than a year. There was no way possible my mother despite her uncommon strength could have taken on the added responsibility of four (making a total of eight additional mouths to feed) more children. Unfortunately Rupert's wife Dana had no one to help her with the children except my mother. This was not a burden that she wished to place on my mother although she knew my mom would jump to the occasion to care for her grandchildren just because of the person she was.

Dana was bi-racial but her mother did not want to be a part of her grandchildren's lives. None of us really understood the nature of her ostracism of Dana or her kids, especially when she pretended to be so tolerant of her daughter's marriage to someone "out of her race". I am again reminded of the total hypocrisy of some people. It is like the pot calling the kettle black. There had to be an occasion, if only once that the color of someone's skin did not make that big of a difference to Dana's mother.

Edith, Dana's mom ignorantly and vehemently denied ever being raped, so you figure this one out. We can always see the mistakes or faults (specks) in others while totally overlooking the beam in our own eyes. The NIV (New International Version) states in Matthew 7:3-5 "Why do you look at the speck of sawdust in your brother's eye and pay no attention to the plank in your own eye? How can you say to your brother, 'Let me take the speck out of your eye,' when all the time there is a plank in your own eye? You hypocrite, first take the plank out of your own eye, and then you will see clearly to remove the speck from your brother's eye."

NEVER THIS WAY AGAIN

It was a miracle and a true gift from God that Rue was able to care for Rosalind's children after she died. Tim, Rosalind's husband, walked away from the marriage and his responsibilities to his children shortly after the birth of their youngest child, making what turned out to still be thirteen kids under one roof after we, her oldest four had moved into homes of our own. My mother, the giant of motherhood, left a heritage of strength and integrity for all of us that defy any manmade perception of motherhood being exercised today.

With just mom and the help from Raymond and myself, who by this time had pretty good jobs, were able to financially lighten the burden on our mother of caring for our sister's children. Not only was she beginning to visibly age, she was becoming noticeably tired and frail. The inner strength she possessed never quenched. However, those closest to her recognized that she was succumbing to the many years of service she had provided for others, most time unappreciated and rarely acknowledged, was now cruelly taking its toll on her physically, but in spite of this fact, her "I can conquer the world" spirit remained intact.

The impact of my siblings deaths, are still felt today but most traumatic of all their deaths was that of Raymond's. He died very mysteriously with suspicious implications. Four hours after leaving the recovery room following a surgery that the doctor had assured his wife of six months and I was routine and that he should, barring no complications be able to go home from the hospital the next day. I won't go into a lot of details, but my brother drowned in his own blood. This was documented in the coroners' report. When asked why no help was gotten for him before his condition became life threatening, his wife told me, "Maybe; they (the nurses) were busy". The recalling of the event, and having been there in the room with him when he passed makes the emotions too "raw" to this date to even talk about Raymond's death, plus the grieving process is only starting. His passing is just that recent.

I miss Raymond the most because a long time after Rosalind and Rupert died we were all we had in the way of family in the part of Michigan where we lived and where I continue to live. My mother made us poignantly aware of this fact just before she died, by telling us that we were all that we had and that we should "look after" one other. That bond remained strong and unchanged between my brother and me until the Lord chose to call him home as well.

Now there's only me left of the "infamous four", and considering my years, I must admit that most times I am very lonely- for immediate family-and uncertain. I do know, or hope that I did get each of my three siblings ready to go home with Jesus. I never failed to tell them about the saving Grace of Jesus Christ, as I also tell my younger siblings, even though my message might have fallen or fall on deaf ears at times. May God forgive me if I have failed either of them?

A lot of my younger siblings do not understand the bond that was between Raymond and me because they weren't there when we had to buy food, or pay a pressing bill for one another when money was short for one of us. They weren't there when we had to pray one another through some difficult situation we were facing either. This is not to say that some of them would not have been in a position to gladly come to the aid of either one of us, but there wasn't the comfort level present with our other siblings that were apparent with Raymond and I allowing us to depend on one another. It was hard for both of us to ask any of our younger siblings for assistance because some of them took pleasure in being able to talk about what they did for someone, especially us, *plus* we were the oldest, and felt they should be able to come to us for help when needed and not the opposite.

I am regrettably recognizing an almost sinful pride that I have stated earlier was instilled in all of us from the time we were old enough to know that we should not ask anyone for anything. We knew that our help came from God and not man, therefore I find it difficult to understand why this feeling is so strong against reaching out to man for help, when I know from scriptures that God works through man on all our behalves.

Even though it is not intentional, I can feel the exclusion some of my younger siblings undoubtedly felt, and is subconsciously demonstrated by their excluding me from some of their less than formal or emergency gatherings on a daily basis, but as stated before, you cannot ask for a closer knit family than we are when it comes to being there for one another when the time for family to unite presents itself.

Raymond wasn't married when our mother passed, but he did get married about a year or so later, and less than a year after his marriage he too, was gone. I'm recognizing some disturbing patterns apparent only after putting my thoughts on paper are they being revealed. Each of their death's (Rosalind, Rupert and Raymond's) suggested that their passing was caused by something other than medical reasons, and perhaps caused by the actions of man, but as previously stated, no action were taken by our family because we were too busy trying to pick up the pieces from each devastating death to bring our family back to some kind of normalcy.

Could this also, as I write, be God's way of bringing about a healing of my distress, and a confirmation of His love for me? It seems; despite the fact, that everyone that I loved intimately, except my three surviving children, seven of my younger siblings, and several grandchildren, nieces and nephews have gone on to be with the Lord. I am continuously recognizing there may indeed be a "pattern" in place finally having to acknowledge a strength in all of us that comes only from God. This strength from God is most apparent when we suffer a loss, specifically through death.

I am in complete amazement with the similarities shared in all four of our lives. We siblings all had four children, two boys and two girls each. Rosalind and Rupert both died at age twenty-five leaving four very small children without a significant, nurturing parent relationship that should have been the foundation for their young lives. Yes, I realize my mother's selfless intervention to provide some continuity in the lives of my sister's children in the absence of their mom, and my brother's wife in the absence of their dad was the closest thing to the children's deceased parents being there but not that of taking the place of the missing parent.

Rue loved her grandchildren unconditionally, but she could never love them the way both their parents would have. The same applied to Rupert's four children. Dana would still be the same dedicated, loving mother she had always been, but now she would have to be both mother and father to her children until the Lord filled the void left by Rupert's death, by someone else.

Our eerie connection as siblings did not end with us having the same number of children or unbreakable blood ties, we all had a strength instilled in us by our mother and grandmother that allowed us to be a source of strength for each other, and more specifically for our mother while painfully watching her children die before her, which she had prayed would never happen. "No parent should ever have to bury a child that is not the expected order of things" would always be her response when asked how she felt after the shock of being told one of her children had died.

Rue denied being anything other than the pillar of strength she was, the one who had to be the comforter instead of the one consistently in need of comforting. This concept of being anything other than the one to do the comforting was totally a foreign concept which was not easily accepted by her.

She was known to possess this strength throughout every loss she experienced. However, she never allowed us to believe that her strength came from anyone or anything but God living in her. I witnessed this strength when my brother Gregory, by my mother's second marriage died of Hodgkin's disease at the age of ten to be followed by the devastation stated earlier of all we held dear when my sister died so suddenly with the brain aneurysm that left four minor, one still in diapers, fatherless children.

Then to have witnessed the stoic, almost emotionless expression on Rue's face when we both were told our children, her son, my brother and my son, had been involved in a freak car accident that had instantly taken both their lives. Little did I know then, but I quickly learned that the pain of losing a child can be so all-consuming it is almost paralyzing when you're first told about the loss especially when you've never lived through such an overwhelming loss in the past. For the very first time, I not only saw my mother, but a woman that has had more than her share of grief and pain, and yet remaining an example of strength that only comes from God. I finally saw who and what my mother was, a woman of God.

I can only thank God that she had gone on before Raymond, thereby being spared the heart wrenching pain of having to bury her fourth child. I do not believe she would have held up with the loss of another child and maintain that pillar of strength façade she had ferociously fought to maintain throughout her life even with God giving her the strength.

The loss of four children, her parents, two husbands had just been too much. I know her faith in God never wavered, but life's brutal knocks and bruises had finally taken its toll. Rue reluctantly accepted her frailties. That is when I saw the inner strength that could have only come from God that allowed her to remain sane when all and everything in her world had taken a disappointing turn, making her accept her vulnerability.

I know without doubt that my siblings' dying in no way was to teach me a lesson of sorts, but I realize that it is God's way of letting me know that even though they are no longer here, I still as always have Him to get me through *anything* that I may encounter. I have been through enough changes, and yes, trauma to know that whenever one thing change, something else begins.

NEVER THIS WAY AGAIN

Therefore I consistently hold onto this evolved concept of renewal. Knowing that the God I serve is omniscient.

Chapter Nineteen: Frailties

I don't know why this concept is so difficult to grasp, especially regarding the situation with my remaining children. I am filled with shame and guilt when I really give my lack of faith in God's promise to be with me always such little credence. It is at these times I count myself greatest among the hypocrites, but I know that the God I serve is a forgiving God and He will not count this against me because I have asked and continue to ask His forgiveness daily for *my* humanness.

In the deepest throes of uncertainty, and yes, sometimes self-pity, I first ask for forgiveness for my lack of trust in our Father God, and then I claim and must rest on the promise found in Hebrews 13:5, when He promises "I will never leave (fail) you or forsake you." Even so, there is still an inner conflict, regarding my inability to shrug off the fact that those still here, that I love and have sacrificed the most for, causes me the *most* inner conflict.

The pain I feel is like looking in my mirror and seeing the one child that tells me he is just like me, then to reflect back on my life when I was trying to "find myself" and see the many frailties and downright stupid mistakes I made all in the guise of developing my own individuality, making some of the things my son did not nearly as dumb as the antics my mother had to put up with while I was going through my growing pangs. I see myself in my two daughters as well. Maybe not in the rebellious ways my son acted out that reminded me of my same behaviors, but in my determination to be my own person, both daughters exhibit some of the same traits and behaviors I was known to possess.

This exercise in bearing my innermost thoughts and emotions is making me really take a genuine look at myself. At what stage in our Christian walk do we just simply "Let go, and let God"? I'm going to be honest with you, as strong as I feel my faith is in the Lord's total control of my life, I still, stubbornly although not always completely aware of this fact, take back a problem time and time again after genuinely feeling that I have "given" the problem to the Lord only having to realize that *here I go again, leaning on my own understanding and not that of the Lord's.*

At what time do we simply accept the fact that God is indeed in control of our very existence, and without this control in our lives, we will inevitably fail no matter how on top of life we foolishly think we are?

This might explain why this past year has been the most difficult I've ever experienced. I have always "tried" to do the *Lords'* business by foolishly believing that *I* can handle any situation without Gods' help, guess what? I always make a mess of an already "sticky" situation thinking I can outdo God. We only learn how very fragile we are when God makes it painfully clear to us that *He* is our only source of strength and help by allowing events in our lives that make us realize how very impotent we are without Him. Then and only then will we cease getting spanked by our Father God for our childish and rebellious behaviors.

At the risk of being redundant, yet again , when will we finally understand that we can do nothing and expect it to be successful without God's favor? Is there a certain learning curve we go through as Christians that finally lets us know we have grown enough spiritually to discern the events of our lives? Probably not, because even with our "cursed" free will and what we like to believe is our being spiritually led, as human beings we are going to make mistakes, *humongous* ones.

The true measure of Christian growth however, is in knowing that we have weaknesses and we're going to make mistakes, and hopefully learn from them, then to ask forgiveness for our trespasses, and doing everything in our power, with God's help, not to repeat the same transgressions again.

I agree, when we are in the "world" the successes we think we have accomplished causing us to feel infallible and overly confident in our own abilities *however sweet, and short lived they are,* these successes of the world are temporary. While we may hold onto all the material trappings success affords, after a while these material "things" are lacking in the true successes that come from the peace and fulfillment God gives us when we experience His promises to love us, to provide for us, to be closer than a brother, and to be a stronghold against the enemy.

These gifts and promises from God are the true measure of success when accepted. The worldly successes we continue to strive for to the extent of omitting God means absolutely nothing when we cannot enjoy these successes because they were acquired via sinful mechanisms and any success we acquire without God is nothing.

By sharing this intimate part of my life with you has made me realize that perhaps some of the separation anxieties I'm experiencing, are a combination of many "feelings" of being abandoned. Although everyone that has gone on to be with the Lord, and I know that if they could have stayed a little longer here with me, they would have, but I still feel a sense of loss, and yes; abandonment by my mother, grandmother, husbands, son, and sister and brothers through no fault of their own except for the desire to shed their earthly garments for eternal vestments.

At any rate, as "now" as these feelings of loss are, regarding those that are no longer here is concerned, I would be remiss if I did not mention God's presence time and time again to cushion the blows and to comfort me, but these losses pales dramatically compared to the rejection felt from my own children that remain here in the land of the living.

Little did I know just two short years ago, the process of what I perceived to be "abandonment" was inevitable, and I guess you're saying, here we go again with the "woe is me", "you have got to feel sorry for me" worn out rhetoric, but I hate to disappoint you.

If I were a died-in-the-wool gambler, I would be willing to bet a nickel against a fly swatter that there is not one of you over fifty years of age that hasn't felt rejected by your children at one time or another. Perhaps, not to the extent that I have, however cautiously, shared with you, but to some degree or another, there is a shared commonality among us whether we are willing to admit it or not. As fragile human beings, we tend to shun anything that makes us look or appear infallible or to have less than the overly high, yet self-perceived opinions we erroneously hold about ourselves. Part of Romans 12:3 states "Do not think of yourself more highly than you ought, but rather think of yourself with sober judgment, in accordance with the measure of faith God has given you."

Chapter Twenty: Friends, We All Have Them

I don't know about any of you, but when I've tried to share my "feelings" with friends (sometimes called fair weather friends) only to have come away with a "Job Complex" has been very disheartening to put it mildly. Although never said, the inference is always there "why don't you get a life?" O.K. to that I say, my life *was* my children. "Now, can you my friend;" I ask, "in all your great wisdom help me to understand why this stage in my life is so difficult to deal with?"

I plead with them to share some of their secrets and wisdom with me as to how they got through this difficult stage of separation from their kids unscathed, yet I'm still admonished to let go, cut the apron strings, kick "em" to the curb, etc. The message was and still is the same "*Get a life*."

I still work a part-time job, I volunteer every opportunity I get, I'm very active in my church and community, so do all these activities qualify as having a life? You tell me. On the surface it would appear so, but there is still an unfulfilled void left by my children's absence that just can't be filled. Let me rephrase that statement, the void is there because there is no longer the closeness, or an inclusion in a life that I feel has excluded me from it.

I am confident, that no one intends or intended to be insensitive, but those "friends" closest to me were and are far from being sensitive. These friends are the ones that constantly refer to my inability to *sever* the apron strings as no more than an overreaction on my part. Some of these *friends* are wonderful, nurturing, God-fearing people who are parents themselves, but these very same advisors allowed their careers and keeping up with the Jones' become the priority that dictated the relationship they had with their children, and at early ages, daycare providers lent a lot to the upbringing of their children.

It is my opinion then and now, that there remains a lot left to be desired when it comes to their being an authority on motherhood and childrearing, especially when they are occupying the seat of judgment regarding how another parent should feel about the anxieties suffered when a child does not live up to a particular expectation as viewed by a parent other than themselves.

If I'm in hot water by making this observation, it is not a condemnation of all parents that work, there are circumstances when a parent *must* work in order to provide in a single-parent family or in other extenuating circumstances. Either way, it is still a parents' decision as to how they will give of themselves to their children and I cannot sit in judgment of them either for the decisions anyone makes or made regarding their children, but neither can a working parent sit in judgment of a parent who chooses to stay home and raise their children. Again, it is a decision that each parent has to make regarding the rearing of his or her children, and it must be a decision either side can live with, without regrets.

Both my mother and grandmother, out of necessity, had no choice but to work outside the home, but their decision to work were to feed us, and not to see how many earthly possessions they could attain. Make no mistake, I know there were times when both of them wished that they could have had the option as to whether they worked or not, but that was not an option given to them. Careers were unheard of for the average woman during their time because most women felt it was their God-given responsibility to stay home and raise their children. My mother and grandmother's decision to work was one of necessity which went against the norms of Christian families during that period in time, but I look back and cannot help but smile because I'm just now realizing, in addition to their many strengths, they were trendsetters as well.

To be fair, the fact that a women stays home with her children will not guarantee that their children will grow up to be more loving and considerate towards them than those of working parents. So when we find it hard to accept the advice of those friends that chose to build careers instead of staying home to raise their children, we must consider *all* the reasons for their decision and not that of what we staunchly perceive to be the only pathway a mother and in rare cases, a father should take to parenthood.

Proverbs 18:24, states it very bluntly based on the premises of my less than sensitive friends when it declares, "There are friends who pretend to be friends, but there is a friend who sticks closer than a brother." That Friend is Jesus Christ. Aren't you glad you have Him as your Lord and Savior, but more importantly, your *Friend?*

I made reference to "fair weather friends" earlier because I have had my share of them. These friends are the ones that are there for you, one hundred percent of the time as long as their perception of you is that of someone that can make them look good, but may God have Mercy if they discover that you cannot or will not allow them to *ride your coattail* to a success they are incapable of achieving themselves. I know this sounds really harsh, but it just proves a point. God does not base His "friendship" towards us predicated on what *we* can do for Him. And let's not ever forget that when Jesus Christ hung on to the cross for the sins of the world, He did not do it for what we could do for Him except to love and serve him, and that is by choice, not demand.

"What a friend we have in Jesus, all our sins and grief to bear" is probably one of the most sung hymns of our time? Not because of the man, Joseph M. Scriven who wrote it as a poem in 1855, but because the words had to have been inspired by God to have such an overwhelming impact on God's people today.

Chapter Twenty-One: Letting Go

Again, this exercise in bearing my innermost thoughts and emotions is making me take a really honest look at myself. Could it be that I am truly not allowing God to have total and complete control in my life? I'm going to be honest with you, even though I feel that my Faith in the Lord is strong enough to withstand the attacks of the enemy, I still find as stated before that as soon as I "give" a problem to God, I somehow take it back time and time again, knowing that each time I rely on my own understanding or misguided ability to solve a particular problem, I make a complete idiot out of myself not because I am dense but because very simply put, I am not following the Will of God.

Simply stated again, every time I try to "fix" an already "sticky" situation you got it, I *mess up* totally and completely. In other words when do we just simply "Let go and let God"? Instead of trying to do something that after a while, especially when there are real and constant reminders that we are not capable of doing anything of substance without Gods' help do we just admit that we are *not* god. As brilliant as we think we are, we still have to admit that we need our Father God to keep us from self-destructing when we try to go it alone without Him.

I guess by now, you are asking yourself, what does everything thus far that I've shared with you have to do with "feeling" that my adult children do not give a rip about me because of their self-absorption? I will tell you. It has everything to do with our perception of how our children do or do not feel. In the first place, although none of us are in the position to read another persons' mind which will allow us to "know" precisely what someone else is truly thinking, but most importantly who are we to try to second-guess God? In other words, "actions speak louder than words." Therefore there is no real argument we can provide that will substitute for the uncaring actions of our children. These *actions* are clear indications that something is not as we would like them to be, and those actions are what we perceive to be *questionable* but are gravely misinterpreted.

Sometimes, as painful as it is the old adage that says, "Action speaks louder than words", is a true statement. Let me give you an example. Again, suppose you are one of the more fortunate parents that have never swallowed the pill of rejection, for whatever reason (we won't go into that) then one day you, to your utter shock and dismay discover that all the love and concern you were receiving from your children just happen to be no more than dull offerings out of a sense of obligation. You would indeed, take another look at how you view their vain offerings of love. But just as importantly, we should honestly reevaluate how we perceive the way our Christian brothers and sisters are handling a situation that we feel is trivial or overly sensitive, but earth shattering to them. Yet we tend to minimize what they are experiencing only because we have *yet* to walk in their shoes.

The statement regarding the valleys our Christian brothers and sisters goes through, only serves to remind us that our personal problems are not unique or exclusive. Maybe after we have examined this fact, then and only then will we know from experience the pain that comes from suddenly realizing that the rose colored glasses we've been looking through has a darker shade that should and will give us pause if we're genuinely honest with ourselves.

I have repeatedly asked God to remove the pain of rejection that I feel, and in its place give me the wisdom to understand why all of us get so busy with our lives that we tend to forget those before us and the sacrifices they made that were once very important in our lives but somehow has lost the significance it once held. I've also asked Him, and continue to do so, to never allow me to become so critical of my brothers and sisters in Christ to the extent that I hide my own inadequacies by shining the light of disclosure brighter on their lives than on my own shortcomings. This is not always an easy task to perform especially when we are often at the brunt end of someone else's insensitivities.

At what time do we forgive ourselves for the insensitive

ways we treated our parents? Or is this the payback that allows us to feel the way we do regarding the "uncaring" ways of our own children? Is this somehow our own self-inflicted punishment for things we did to hurt our parents that we simply cannot forgive ourselves for? Are we expecting too much from our children? All these questions are haunting me as I try to figure out why I am hurting so much. I know without doubt that God has forgiven me for not honoring my mother and grandmother as I should have, and I also know that both of them forgave my less than charitable ways towards them, because that was the way they were – forgiving to a fault, but now my constant prayer, and it is a big one, is that God will help me to forgive myself.

    The greatest war I've ever waged is with me when I try to justify some dumb mistake I've made regarding a sensitive issue revolving around my built-in perceptions of life and how everyone should adhere to my particular point of view. Then, after life has thoroughly kicked my hinny, I then turn with "tail tucked between my legs" to the only source of comfort I know, and that is God, begging for His forgiveness. There's times when I feel like I really do not deserve to be forgiven because, may God help me, I'm only going to repeatedly make the same dumb mistakes over and over again when it comes to trying to manipulate the events in the lives of my children.

    I have beaten myself up so many times for not being more

NEVER THIS WAY AGAIN

sensitive to the needs of my mother and grandmother, and even my dad who is still alive living in North Carolina, that I'm beginning to wonder if I will ever find peace, or a semblance of peace that will help me forgive myself. Now that they are gone, I cannot go to them and ask their forgiveness, so I continue to punish myself by transferring their pain onto myself, which unfortunately makes me really believe this is the crux of my dilemma. Thank God there is still time, however short that I can show my dad the caring and involvement in my life that was missing in my mother and grandmother's life.

Chapter Twenty-Two: Out to Pasture

I will now qualify a statement that I made earlier regarding those precious loved ones that are in nursing homes. I will also state at the onset, that this is not a blanket indictment against all adult children that have had to place elderly parents in nursing homes or assisted care facilities. Again, there are extenuating circumstances that warrant the placement of a loved one, and the bottom line is, the matter is really between the "placing party" and God.

I had to place my second husband in a nursing home but we thought it was just for rehabilitation, little did we know that the idea of abandonment and his feeling that he wasn't needed anymore caused a ripple effect of negative behavior. He became combative, physically lashing out at everyone including his daughter and me. He then had to be sedated with strong narcotics to calm him down, but these narcotics given to him against the family's wishes had a life-altering and damaging effect on him. He became depressed and finally, almost catatonic and within less than one months' time he was dead.

He had many serious health problems, so I am not saying that his being placed in a nursing home was the only cause of his death, but until that placement he had not given up on life, therefore his death was very unexpected and guilt is trying to rear its ugly head again because he begged my daughter and me not to put him in a nursing home, but we convinced him that his stay there was only for rehabilitation and it would be for a very short period of time, depending on his cooperation with the medical staff which was responsible for his speedy recovery. He agreed to the terms as explained to him to be admitted, but something went desperately wrong. Instead of being physically rehabilitated, he died.

So I know firsthand the myriad of emotions involved when it comes to placing a loved one in a nursing home where the residents are more often than not overly sedated as a form of "babysitting". In most facilities where the elderly are cared for, they are unfortunately and commonly understaffed. A problem, regardless of genuine efforts on the part of administrators and medical staff alike, is still an ongoing concern which has not experienced an acceptable solution yet.

This shortage of caretakers could be the lack of decent wages paid to the few that are truly dedicated to the profession, coupled with the fact that one nurse's aide has to care for up to twelve to fifteen patients at a time when they're working an understaffed shift. After a while, no matter how caring this aide is, a certain amount of burnout occurs and the aide unfortunately starts to take short cuts in the care for her patients. This observation is in no way making excuses for the less than quality care our elderly receive, but it is a glimpse into why it is happening. Whatever the variables involved are that allow for less than quality care for those that have paved the way for a majority of us, should be addressed immediately.

The absence of genuine caring for the elderly in today's society by those that remain in the health care field, specifically the professionals dealing with the geriatric population, have lost their compassion for the elderly, perhaps due to the "disposable, what feels good" mentality that allows a society to dispose of, or to replace a people that are perceived to have lost their usefulness, without the slightest feeling of guilt for not being bothered with a situation that doesn't make one "feel" good or one that does not contribute to a perceived standard of living that is the norm for *that* particular day.

I am personally appalled with this prevailing attitude of uncaring, and the acceptance of a situation that places such little importance on a human beings' life just because they've gotten old and cannot contribute in an expected manner. This prevailing attitude is truly deplorable. As much as I cringe at the thought, one day I might be placed in a nursing home, and God forbid if things have not gotten any better by then with reference to the inhumane way residents are treated, I too will experience firsthand the indignities suffered by some of the less fortunate residents in one of these understaffed, seemingly uncaring facilities.

As stated earlier, there are some very caring people still working in these facilities, and there are also some exceptionally well-managed places, but money seems to dictate the quality of care received. The more money one has, the better the care received. I realize this is not a truth that is readily accepted, but true just the same.

Before and after I graduated from college, I worked and continued to work with the elderly, in one capacity or another until a few of years ago. It was in that environment that I experienced firsthand the heart-breaking expressions on the resident's faces and in their not so cleverly disguised teary eyes questioning why they were there, and the utter defeat silently expressed in those same eyes knowing that they no longer had a choice in the matter when it came to making decisions regarding where they would spend the rest of their lives. I prayed fervently that God would make His presence and love for those few residents more apparent than they had ever experienced before.

God's presence would have filled the emptiness that most of these residents felt if only they would have accepted God's gift of comfort instead of the feelings of anger and abandonment some experienced despite a rigid denial by them that they were anything but angry which was harbored by many, but again, pride kept them from admitting to having feelings that they did in fact know from experience the heartbreaking side of rejection and profound loneliness.

    I do not make reference to those that were either physically or mentally challenged to the extent that they no longer possessed their own faculties, but the reference *is clearly* made to those that still had a lot to contribute to society, but because they would have been too much of a bother to care for in one of their children's home, they were placed where they could "die" among people their own age. I was and to a degree am still angry, not so much at the uncaring way I perceived the residents to be treated, although there was and continues to be a major concern for them, there was and is a subconscious fear that is not totally unfounded for the way I feel I will eventually be treated if or when I'm placed in an institution so blatantly uncaring with no room (or expectations) for an immediate solution.

    Thank God there were only a few residents fitting this description, but for those few, my heart still bleeds when I mentally picture and remember the absolute pain in their eyes when either they or someone else would ask about the involvement with their negligent families. Again, and I cannot emphasize this fact enough, we belong to a larger family and that is the family of God, therefore our disappointments and sadness is only temporary while here, but it is such a sad commentary on the way our loved ones are treated just because they've outlived a perceived usefulness.

NEVER THIS WAY AGAIN

We must take comfort in not only letting our loved ones know that as a member of God's family we will someday know absolute love and happiness, but it is our duty to let them know God has placed in our lives the absolute knowledge of His love for us *right now*. I also know, in our humanness we would rather have a tangible expression of this love, and as hard as it is to accept at times, for some it is the only comfort available outside of those we've been entrusted to for our care in the remaining days of our lives here on earth.

I could cite some disturbing examples, and statistically, these examples would be so common, that it would not violate anyone's confidentiality or shock anyone for that matter, but exposing further an already "sensitive" area regarding the care of our loved ones would amount to no more than "beating a dead horse". Thank God, in nursing homes and convalescing centers there are and continuously employ improved checks and balances that ensure the humane treatment of our loved ones unfortunate enough to have to be placed outside of a familial setting, which may someday improve the lot of our elderly parents not blessed with a bank account the size of the vaults housing all the gold at Fort Knox.

I had always felt that by my providing compassionate, and loving care to the residents as I felt compelled to do, would somehow ensure that when I got "old" or could no longer do for myself someone would show me the same love and compassion that

I without hesitation showed those in my charge. At least that is what I told myself. In my heart, then and now, I did not see myself ever having to go to a nursing home, nor is that a reality now. I felt then that "my" children would always be there for me and that "they" would never cause me to suffer the humiliation of being anyplace other than my own home or one of theirs. That belief was then, but now, I seriously and painfully have had to rethink this issue.

I do not make this assertion because I feel my children no longer love me, but I have to unselfishly realize that there may in fact be circumstances that will prevent them from "taking care" of me as I would want them to when I can no longer do for myself. Like most parents, I pray that I will not outlive my usefulness. A usefulness that will ensure my independence until God calls me home is perhaps a bit overly optimistic, but a prayer and a desire I yearn for all the same.

There is always the indisputable fact that we all must acknowledge and it is that Our Father God, has ultimate control over each and every one of us, and not one of us can determine if we live one hour or fifty years from the time we awake each day. Everything is in God's hand no matter what or how we pray that things might be different especially when it is according to our own selfish desires.

Chapter Twenty-Three: Conflicts-All My Children

My two daughters Kay, the older of the two and the youngest Shanna, have their own set of concerns, values and issues. Kay's husband Luke is an excellent provider, but very controlling. Her faith in God is very strong, which allows her to stay in a relationship that anyone not rooted in the sound doctrines of Christ would have left years ago. When cornered, she would always quote 1 Peter 3:1 "Wives, in the same way be submissive to your husbands so that, if any of them do not believe the word, they may be won over without words by the behavior of their wives." I don't know if her adherence to this particular precept from God's word was for her benefit and survival or mine to help me understand why she stayed in a marriage that was void of the love we all expect to be the foundation of our marriages.

God has however, shown this daughter special *Favor* because she has had to overcome situations that were very abusive both physical and emotional, yet she endured all she went through in silence. I did not find out about some of the more disturbing incidents in her life until they had almost been resolved. I cannot stop thanking God for the hedge of protection that was around her during the early years of her marriage. I also, wonder why our relationship wasn't one that would allow her to let me know she was in an abusive relationship. I am not going to second guess what her reasons were at the time, but I am certain that her not wanting me to know that her marriage was less than perfect was one of the reasons she felt she could not confide in me, and did not, until much later in her marriage when the abuse had subsided somewhat. She only had to contend with verbal abuse and not both physical and verbal abuse as she had put up with when her children were younger.

She was determined to stay home and raise her four children in the church as mandated by her Christian beliefs, but as we have talked, she has confided in me that all her children are also self-centered and uncaring at times especially the youngest daughter and son, despite the sacrifices and less than ideal circumstances she endured in order to honor her role as a stay at home mother to them. This revelation reinforces a documented statement made earlier when I stated that the way our children turn out is not dependent on whether a parent decides to work outside the home or stay at home and raise their children.

It is still a parental preference to pursue a career or not, but it is a biblical preference for a mother to stay at home and raise the children. Kay was a devoted stay at home mother, but that did not alter the outcome of her children to be any different than those of working parents when it came to their being self-absorbed and incredibly self-serving.

NEVER THIS WAY AGAIN

Again, I will say that I simply do not understand this phenomenon of self-absorption in our children today. Maybe this cruel realization has always been an active yet disheartening presence in the lives of some, if not all parents since the beginning of time. Whatever the dynamics involved are, it is truly a sad commentary we as parents must accept, especially when all that we perceive as parents is the utterly uncaring ways of our children, just may be a repayment for how we treated our parents. Anything is possible, but I pray this self-pleasuring attitude our children have is a phase that goes away as they age. Time will tell because as each of us has gotten older, we too had to change and become the mature, caring adults we'd like to think we have become.

Kay has always let me know that she loves me and would do anything for me, but because she lives in another state, we only visit via telephone unless on certain occasions when I go back to North Carolina or she comes to visit me here in Michigan. She has also asked me to move to North Carolina to be close to her and my grandchildren, and while I would love to do just that, my life is here in Michigan where I have established a life surrounded with people that give my life what little meaning it has left without the inclusion of all parts of my children's lives, although this may be a little selfish at times on my part to make changes at this late stage in my life, I have given the decision to move or to stay here in Michigan to God, so whatever He wants me to do, this is what I will do.

NEVER THIS WAY AGAIN

My youngest daughter Shanna, the baby of my brood has chronic health problems that present continuous challenges for her at all times, but of all my children, she has the strongest determination to take life's lemons and make lemonade by not allowing her illness to prevent her from enjoying all that life has to offer. Most people with Shanna's illness would settle for the inevitability of getting disability for the rest of their lives and leave it at that, but she has stubbornly and courageously responded to this cop-out to life's unfairness with a resounding NO by completing college and working every day that her health would permit, and we both thank God she has a job that is understanding and tolerant of her health issues.

Shanna has a rare blood disease, which was diagnosed at birth that has no possibility of a cure unless and until God decides to heal her. We both are firm believers in God's ability to heal and prayerfully await this blessed event to come to fruition before we leave this place, but if God decides not to heal Shanna, we also know that there is a reason, a reason that will ultimately bring glory to his name.

Shanna also has a beautiful daughter that is blessed with the same determination to be the best in everything she attempts. Raelynn has consciously made every effort, even from a very young age to make her mom proud and to validate the gift given to both of them in their abilities to overcome whatever obstacle presented to them. There is present in Raelynn a strength that is uncommon in children her age, but first we have to acknowledge that this strength is from God, yet it is also due to the fact that this young child, now age ten, has had to adapt to the many stays in the hospital her mom has had and continues to unfortunately have, which has forced her to adjust to keeping long hours in the hospital with her mom, and being away from her home during these bouts of hospitalizations.

This has built a character in her that is rare in most adults. Of course I have been and will be there for both of them throughout every incident, but my presence does not make up for the times Raelynn has to be away from her mother under conditions neither of them have control of. But through it all, each of us has learned to depend on our Father, God to safeguard and strengthen us through every crisis we experience every time Shanna has to be hospitalized. My daughter Shanna has a home that she keeps beautifully in spite of her physical limitations. One could compare it with some of the homes on display in one of the more popular magazines displaying beautiful homes. Everything Shanna does is done with such determination it is amazing that she finds the energy to perform them. She is a very visible parent in her daughter's school making sure Raelynn gets the best academically her school has to offer.

Shanna's decision not to marry the father of her child was not a decision made lightly. She sought God's forgiveness first for becoming pregnant before marriage, and then weighing all the

NEVER THIS WAY AGAIN

My youngest daughter Shanna, the baby of my brood has chronic health problems that present continuous challenges for her at all times, but of all my children, she has the strongest determination to take life's lemons and make lemonade by not allowing her illness to prevent her from enjoying all that life has to offer. Most people with Shanna's illness would settle for the inevitability of getting disability for the rest of their lives and leave it at that, but she has stubbornly and courageously responded to this cop-out to life's unfairness with a resounding NO by completing college and working every day that her health would permit, and we both thank God she has a job that is understanding and tolerant of her health issues.

Shanna has a rare blood disease, which was diagnosed at birth that has no possibility of a cure unless and until God decides to heal her. We both are firm believers in God's ability to heal and prayerfully await this blessed event to come to fruition before we leave this place, but if God decides not to heal Shanna, we also know that there is a reason, a reason that will ultimately bring glory to his name.

Shanna also has a beautiful daughter that is blessed with the same determination to be the best in everything she attempts. Raelynn has consciously made every effort, even from a very young age to make her mom proud and to validate the gift given to both of them in their abilities to overcome whatever obstacle presented to them. There is present in Raelynn a strength that is uncommon in children her age, but first we have to acknowledge that this strength is from God, yet it is also due to the fact that this young child, now age ten, has had to adapt to the many stays in the hospital her mom has had and continues to unfortunately have, which has forced her to adjust to keeping long hours in the hospital with her mom, and being away from her home during these bouts of hospitalizations.

This has built a character in her that is rare in most adults. Of course I have been and will be there for both of them throughout every incident, but my presence does not make up for the times Raelynn has to be away from her mother under conditions neither of them have control of. But through it all, each of us has learned to depend on our Father, God to safeguard and strengthen us through every crisis we experience every time Shanna has to be hospitalized. My daughter Shanna has a home that she keeps beautifully in spite of her physical limitations. One could compare it with some of the homes on display in one of the more popular magazines displaying beautiful homes. Everything Shanna does is done with such determination it is amazing that she finds the energy to perform them. She is a very visible parent in her daughter's school making sure Raelynn gets the best academically her school has to offer.

Shanna's decision not to marry the father of her child was not a decision made lightly. She sought God's forgiveness first for becoming pregnant before marriage, and then weighing all the variables regarding all the pluses and minus' a relationship with the child's father would involve after discovering some really negative habits he had, decided after much prayer and counsel from our pastor that she would be better off not marrying him considering their relationship would add more stress to her life, stress that would ultimately cause damage to her already fragile health in major proportions.

Those that are "holier than thou" asked why didn't she see these negative traits and habits in her child's father before she got pregnant and all we could tell them is that if *they* were without sin, let them cast the first stone. Her situation was not condoned because sin is sin, but isn't it wonderful we're not dependent on man for forgiveness. Only God can and will forgive sin.

There is however a dark side to Shanna. She is her father's daughter. As much as I would like to take credit for her industrious, get ahead determination, I see a lot of her father in her when it comes to stepping on anyone that gets in her way when she wants to accomplish something. She sees this behavior as not "being weak" This concerns me greatly because when she's in this mode of getting things done, she seems to not care who she hurts. I only hope these negative traits and actions won't rub off on her daughter. The bottom line is, she keeps me on my knees, not only for her physical health, but for her spiritual health as well.

My son Ron, my third born, let's just say he keeps me on my knees *overtime*. Only God has stayed his life because He knows that my son and His child is somewhere deep within the person my son Ron has unfortunately become due to the sinful trappings of this world. My heart breaks to see what and who my surviving son has become and it scares me all the time for fear that I will lose him as I did my first-born. My constant prayer is that God will save him and spare his life, because as I constantly remind God of something He needs no reminder of, Ron "cannot serve Him from the grave".

I also see the daily struggles Ron has trying to get a handle on what must be an insurmountable problem of drug addiction. In addition to the many problems he faces in general coping with life daily, there is always the constant reminder that he can never really succeed because the enemy has such an unrelenting grasp on his life, or so he thinks, that it causes him to just gives up at times, not even trying to get victory over his addiction or other life altering situations, which have prevented him from receiving a victory that is only available to him through Christ Jesus.

If only Ron would slow down long enough to let God heal him, his battles would not make him feel he's so completely alone most of the time. No amount of encouraging or displays of love he is shown seems to help, he still cannot grasp the reality that God will indeed cure him of his addiction if he would only believe Our Father when He promises, "with the strips Jesus received", he too can be healed. 1 Peter 2:24

Needless to say, Ron, in spite of the God given strengths and gifts he is blessed with, has allowed his addiction to take complete control of his life preventing him from using his many talents a great amount of the time. His struggles have been a constant battle for both of us, because the enemy takes great joy in destroying those who are most vulnerable, as my son Ron is.

As a mother I see and feel the pain and struggles he is going through. As a black, male child with an addiction coupled with a criminal record, society has labeled him as a failure already before finding out why he has the strikes against him. If I could take away the pain that his addiction has almost crippled him with, I would without hesitation bear his burdens just to give him a chance to experience life as God has destined all of his children to enjoy, if only for a moment.

Looking back, as stated previously, Ron has been the one child that demanded our undivided attention. If he could not get the attention desired in a positive manner, he would invent ways, even if they were negative to get the attention he wanted. Both his dad and I have to take responsibility for not being there for him when we should have been regardless of the reasons we've tried to tell ourselves we had.

NEVER THIS WAY AGAIN

No amount of prayer or therapy seemed to help at the time, and you can only guess the guilt I felt because I did not know what made this child behave as he did or what I may or may not have contributed to bring about his negative behavior. Did I not show him that I loved him enough? Did I somehow miss a crucial message he was trying to tell his dad and I that may have caused him to feel less than what God intended for him to feel about his life and its purpose? I know without doubt that Ron loves God, but he questions why God has allowed the enemy to take such a relentless hold on his life as he has helplessly, without the will at times to fight the enemy; have falsely accused God of not being there for him. This is when my child is at his lowest point. This is also the time, as his mother that my heart bleeds the most for him.

I have been cautioned against taking ownership for Ron's negative behavior, but as his mother, I feel I could have done more to help him escape the torment he is now suffering. I will always feel that I did not do enough to lessen his pain. Yes, I sought every possible remedy available to help my son, but all my efforts seemed to hit a brick wall when it came to actually making a positive difference in Ron's life, may God have mercy on the both of us.

All of my children, in my prejudiced opinion, are some of the most gifted and talented children on this planet. It is no exaggeration when I state unashamedly that my son Ron is the most multi-talented of the three. I have promised him that I will help him with a book he is writing, and I have also agreed to help him get recognition for his awesome paintings, two of which are really good and deserving of more kudos than I, his mother have been able to lavish on him, which he so richly deserves, I might add. I somehow cannot find the words to adequately express my genuine pride in his accomplishments in a way that would make him value himself enough to find the strength to fight his addiction and other demons.

As stated previously, and please forgive me if I seem to continue to boast, but God *has* blessed all of my children with very great and unique talents. Kay and Ron both have the voices of angels, and not only can they sing, they also write some of the songs they sing. All three of my children have the gift of expressing themselves through the written word as well. As previously stated, Ron is an artist and he signs all his works with 'by R.P Gifted Hands.' This signature represents validation that God inspires all that he does.

Shanna is the chef in the family. She can prepare and present award-winning dishes rivaled by none, but her specialty is baked goods. Her dream is to have her own catering business in the near future. We both discovered her talent to bake at about age nine when she made a pineapple upside down cake from scratch. To my amazement, she had watched and absorbed information from cooking shows, which highlighted specialty-baked goods when most kids her age were watching cartoons or some other shows catering to kids only, she was like a sponge absorbing everything the great chef's had to offer in order to perfect her talent.

This talent has only gotten better as time has progressed. Her desire to have a catering business of her own also comes from the need to be as independent as possible, not having to answer to a boss when her health is an issue. Her plan is to employ and train others to run the business in her absence, although the need to have someone else run her business will not be something that is a constant occurrence, she feels it will be a wise business decision to employ these strategies.

These are just some of the talents and gifts from God that could make all my children independently wealthy but who can understand the foolishness of youth. Their tomorrows are forever, or so they think, never seriously giving thought that old age is just around the corner for them as well, and everything that is put off today may not necessarily be able to "get done" tomorrow. If only we as parents, could get this very real truth through to our children.

I'm going to dispel a myth at the outset because I do not want to come across as this controlling, unyielding, shrew of a mother that is only concerned with what my adult children can or should do for me as repayment for "all" I've done for them, just the opposite. I am honored that God saw fit, to bless me with four beautiful, talented children. I am also thankful to God that He allowed all of them to make it to adulthood except my oldest son, Lavan age fourteen when he was killed in the auto accident with my brother Rupert whom I made reference to earlier. To have raised them to maturity, with all its many challenges, is still considered a blessing, which I am eternally grateful to God for. Perhaps when those children remaining, and are much older, they will begin to appreciate all the "favor" God has shown them during their lives, as I now do.

Having said all this, does it make the sense of rejection and abandonment any less painful or real? Absolutely not! This inner conflict is maddening. On one hand, I know that God can fix this problem for me, but on the other hand, I just *don't know how to let Him do it*. I've asked everyone in the universe (that's stretching it a bit) to pray for me, but again, I *know* that I have to stop trying to solve this problem of feeling rejected by my children myself and let God do it, then to finally accept the basic truth that God is my only *true* source of strength during this painful process of adjustment in my life is still disconcertingly present.

All the prayers in the world, by everyone in the world, will not do one iota of good, if I (we) do not adhere to the Will of God. Keeping in mind that it is not God's Will that any of His children should suffer. If I could realistically count the times I have gone through unnecessary situations that have truly made me suffer, it would surprise many, but none of the things I went through was unavoidable. I suffered because I did not follow the leading of the Holy Spirit; therefore it is never God's Will but our own that forces us to go through unnecessary trials and tribulations brought about by our own stiff-necked, and more often than not, disobedient behavior and attitudes.

The Apostle Paul perhaps explains in Romans 7:15-20 why we are disobedient at times when he wrote "I do not understand what I do. For what I want to do I do not do, but what I hate I do. And if I do what I do not want to do, I agree that the law is good. As it is, it is no longer I myself that do it, but it is sin living in me. I know that nothing good lives in me, that is, in my sinful nature. For I have the desire to do what is good but, I cannot carry it out. For what I do is not the good I want to do; no, the evil I do not want to do-this I keep on doing. Now if I do what I do not want to do, it is no longer I who do it, but it is sin living in me that does it." NIV

The Apostle Paul in no way gives us license to sin, but he helps us all know that our constant war to do right is spiritual as well as carnal.

Chapter Twenty-Four: Children, A Gift

Does this suffering and pain of rejection and abandonment come from the fact that we are not *honestly* willing to "let go" of our children? Do we look at them as being our personal property? Is this a phenomenon experienced by a parent not having the support and reassurance of the other partner on the parenting team? These are more questions that beg to be answered, if for no other reason than to bring some clarity to my own understanding of the failures on my part to deal with what I consider to be the "put out to pasture" syndrome by my children long before I feel that I'm ready, if anyone ever is ready for this finality in one's life, need to be answered.

I have alluded to the fact that I probably would be able to deal more effectively with my children's uncaring attitudes and acts if one of their father's had been here to be a support system for me, but this is not a reality. They are both, hopefully in Heaven. But even if one of them were still alive, I'm not sure there would be the type of support available that is needed, which brings me right back to the irrefutable truth that God is my only source of support and eventual healing from this pain of feeling such intense abandonment.

NEVER THIS WAY AGAIN

I count it a blessing and an honor to have been given the opportunity to be a mother especially when there are so many women for whatever reason are unable to bear children. Some women are barren at birth, while others are unable to bear children for medical conditions that made them infertile with or without their knowledge, but each of these scenarios leaves the women unable to have children,. These women want no more than to just experience what every woman God put on earth will feel, and that is to experience life in the womb, to hold that newborn infant for the first time after the birth, knowing that the child is hers, and he or she is the ultimate gift from God, this is an experience that no woman should have to miss unless she makes a conscience decision never to have children.

Then you have those mothers that for one reason or another, leaves most of us with the question as to why the bonding that is inherent in most mothers is unfortunately missing in these, thankfully few women. Try as they may that glorious gift of motherhood escapes their comprehension. The sense of detachment is a pervasive and all-encompassing emotion, if one could call this *unnatural* feeling an emotion. Getting pregnant, having the child means no more to them than being inconvenienced for nine months *if* they choose to have the child.

There are even less than honorable instances of women having children for the sole purpose of getting *paid* for their "contribution" to someone unable to have children. I won't go into that issue because it is a problem or situation that our Father God will deal with according to the circumstances that brought about the unfortunate conditions and/or situations.

There are other situations when a woman will use abortion as a form of birth control. Whether their decision to abort the child was because they made a "mistake" for medical reasons, or if they were simply misinformed about the sanctity of life depending at which stage one believes life begins. The act of abortion begs to be understood by those of us that know "God knew us in the womb." But knowing this, we have to accept the fact that everyone has made mistakes, and no one is perfect except our Father God and His Son Jesus Christ. Therefore we must remember that when we judge someone, the Lord will judge us accordingly.

It is just my position that these children that never got a chance to have gotten here may have loved their mothers and fathers unconditionally and would have cared for them in their declining years. Unfortunately only God knows how any of these scenarios could or would have turned out. Ultimately, it is God's business and not ours, but we still must call sin what it is, and abortion is considered by many to be one of *many* sins.

Again, it is not my place to judge the moral tenets of these issues because as stated, only God can judge another human being.

However, usually when these situations occur there is an absence of a personal relationship with God in the lives of those who place so little value on another human beings life whether they are born or not.

While they may *know of* God, they *do not know* God. We can rest assured that God wants to have a personal relationship with all of us, and it is not that God Himself has made His presence unavailable to us; He simply and sadly has not been invited into the lives of those where His presence is missing.

Revelation 3:20 states "Behold I stand at the door, and knock; if any man hear my voice, and open the door, I will come in to him, and will sup with him, and he with Me" but as God Himself has stated, we must ask Him to come into our lives. As much as God loves us, He will never force Himself on us. This is probably one of the most important values and mandates from God's word that we as parents should instill into the lives of our children. If we neglect such an important word from God, by not making it mandatory that our children understand this tenet, we can only expect the uncaring attitudes some our children have when life-sustaining directives from God are ignored.

To quote Proverbs 22:6 again, we are to "Train up a child in the way he should go: and when he is old, he will not depart from it." We all had to be told about God's saving Grace from the knee up. As parents it is our responsibility to let our children know without uncertainty about the saving grace of our Lord and Savior, Jesus Christ and the enormity of that cost paid for us. In my case, and in the lives of my children, this truth was never one to be debated, it was an accepted truth and way of life. God however, through His infinite wisdom allows us the choice as to how or if we accept this truth. I'm forever grateful for God's Holy Word, in its entirety which is all the truth we will ever need.

At no time was there ever a question as to whether we should or should not accept this truth, but there have been times I wonder if my children may at times, forget, ever so briefly, the truths taught to them as little ones and throughout their formative years, and whether these truths are still operative in their lives today. It is however, my constant prayer that my children will not depart from the directions and training they received at my knees and if they do, as God's word so clearly states, they *will not* depart from lessons taught to them for any length of time, lessons on truths which will be a tradition to teach their children in return.

There is one tradition that the Lord gave me to instill in my children at very early ages. To give an example of this tradition, which they all have taken into adulthood, is that every New Year before the celebration begins, each of them are on their knees giving thanks to God for blessing them to see yet another year. This is not to say that they do not go out later and celebrate the New Year in the sometimes, unpopular but traditional way the world celebrates, but it is evident that they have not departed from a tradition that was also instilled in them at very early ages that they still honor.

My son Ron called me from jail where he was spending time for driving without or on an expired or suspended license and proudly told me that he had just gotten off his knees thanking God for letting him live to see another year. While it always hurt me when he was locked-up, I did however get a small measure of comfort knowing that God was still a big part of his life. If only he would remember and consciously practice *all* that was instilled in him as a child *before* he makes bad decisions. I just have to remind myself that God is still in control of *everything*.

Our Father God has also made a promise to us and our children when He declared" If thy children will keep my covenant and my testimony that I shall teach them, their children shall also sit upon thy throne for evermore" Psalms 132:12. This was a promise The Lord made to King David, "A man after His own heart". While our children today will not sit on a literal throne nor wear a crown, unless you live in a country that is still ruled by kings and queens, they will be blessed nonetheless when they keep the Lord's covenants. The commandment that comes to mind again as stated at the beginning of this work found in Exodus 20:12 admonishing us to "Honor thy father and mother: that thy days may be long upon the land which the Lord thy God giveth thee" is a commandment with promise, if only we obey it.

Do you suppose that I am taking this "abandonment crisis" too personally out of a sense of fear? Am I being unrealistic in expecting my children to acknowledge me even when they don't need something? Can I honestly say that I raised them to honor me, their mother and other older adults? Or is this (their uncaring ways) my punishment for not correcting my children more firmly when they were less than respectful to their fathers? I am reminded of God's word that says "Be not deceived; God is not mocked: for whatsoever a man soweth, that shall he also reap." Galatians 6:7. We cannot adhere to some of Gods' commands and casually ignore the rest of them.

I can only acknowledge and accept the painful fact that if I am now reaping what I've sown, is it because of the thoughtless and self-absorbed demeanor I exhibited towards my mother and grandmother at times? In my own defense, I was not aware that I was being any way other than a thoughtful daughter and granddaughter, the fact that I was overwhelmed with the living of a very demanding and hurried life which was pulling me in more directions than I was able to keep up with, made me totally unaware of the pain I was emotionally inflicting on them, but now I know from the actual experience of walking in their shoes because now those very shoes are literally being worn on my feet.

Chapter Twenty-Five: Reality Check

This self-analysis or better yet, an unadulterated soul search is designed to help me evaluate the part I've played in what I have unashamedly called abandonment and rejection by my children. Under normal circumstances, my pride would not have allowed me to expose such a vulnerable part of my life to the entire world, but God has a plan for this self- examination. A plan that will allow other parents to really ask themselves if their children were brought up acknowledging God's *Will* for them, or were they raised adhering to Dr. Spock's will?

Little did I know when I began this journey into trying to understand my feelings did I realize that so much had been pent up inside that needed to come out in order to bring about a healing. As an adult, I have never experienced the extreme pangs of poverty that we endured as children, but some of the life lessons I learned during that time has equipped me with values and the where-with-all to deal with just about anything life may throw my way, that is, anything except the feeling of being "abandoned" by my kids. I don't believe anything in life prepares us for the totally unexpected pain that ensues from such a startling revelation.

NEVER THIS WAY AGAIN

Now that both my husbands are deceased, even the minimal moral support expected, as the other member of the parental support team received from them, as the father figures for our children is gone. Could having to bear these feelings of not being needed any more by my children be less painful if I had one of their dads' to share this unsettling time in my life with me? Then again, isn't this the ultimate goal we as parents have, to make our children independent enough to go out into the world and make it on their own without having to come to mom (and or dad) for everything? The last part of 2 Corinthians 12:14 states that "Children ought not to lay up for their parents, but the parents for their children." In other words, we should live our lives, as parents in such a way that the examples we set for our children should in most instances, be the catalyst for modeling independent living for their children in addition to the many other life sustaining lessons required to make their lives more meaningful and less chaotic.

Having said all that, profound as it may sound, it still hurts like the dickens to have done such a great job in raising our kids, having them turn out exactly as we had hoped and prayed they would, especially when they demonstrate on a daily basis that they do not need us any more, does something to our psyches. By them not being fully aware of their ability to make us feel unneeded, proves even further the fantastic job of raising them that we did. What a cruel oxymoron.

NEVER THIS WAY AGAIN

When the Lord said "We will reap what we sow", He meant just that. We cannot treat our parents with disrespectful, uncaring tokens of love and expect our own children to be our forever, faithful servants. I can vividly remember telling my son that I wished he would have not one, but two children identical to him and the way he behaves. This is not to say he is the only one that has been a source of contention for me, but he has demanded the most attention. My very vocal and sincere wish for him was and still is my way of letting him know that with children just like him, he will receive the same treatment he has dished out. Does any of this strike you as Deja Vu? My mother said the exact same words to me. Now I know.

My wish for retribution in his life was just that, a wish. I love him too much to see him suffer the pain he inflicted on me. In my heart, as a mother, I know that none of the things he does is intentional, but because of a number of negative habits which has caused him to become callous, and sometimes even verbally cruel, prevents him from temporarily being the son I raised and know still lives deep within him. Plus, God has not given up on him, why should I? That question does not need to be answered, because for me and parents like me, there is no way we would ever give up on something we birthed into this world, and could, although not acknowledged, be the source of their failure to see the pain they cause us, simply because of the way we raised them.

Now that both my husbands are deceased, even the minimal moral support expected, as the other member of the parental support team received from them, as the father figures for our children is gone. Could having to bear these feelings of not being needed any more by my children be less painful if I had one of their dads' to share this unsettling time in my life with me? Then again, isn't this the ultimate goal we as parents have, to make our children independent enough to go out into the world and make it on their own without having to come to mom (and or dad) for everything? The last part of 2 Corinthians 12:14 states that "Children ought not to lay up for their parents, but the parents for their children." In other words, we should live our lives, as parents in such a way that the examples we set for our children should in most instances, be the catalyst for modeling independent living for their children in addition to the many other life sustaining lessons required to make their lives more meaningful and less chaotic.

Having said all that, profound as it may sound, it still hurts like the dickens to have done such a great job in raising our kids, having them turn out exactly as we had hoped and prayed they would, especially when they demonstrate on a daily basis that they do not need us any more, does something to our psyches. By them not being fully aware of their ability to make us feel unneeded, proves even further the fantastic job of raising them that we did. What a cruel oxymoron.

NEVER THIS WAY AGAIN

When the Lord said "We will reap what we sow", He meant just that. We cannot treat our parents with disrespectful, uncaring tokens of love and expect our own children to be our forever, faithful servants. I can vividly remember telling my son that I wished he would have not one, but two children identical to him and the way he behaves. This is not to say he is the only one that has been a source of contention for me, but he has demanded the most attention. My very vocal and sincere wish for him was and still is my way of letting him know that with children just like him, he will receive the same treatment he has dished out. Does any of this strike you as Deja Vu? My mother said the exact same words to me. Now I know.

My wish for retribution in his life was just that, a wish. I love him too much to see him suffer the pain he inflicted on me. In my heart, as a mother, I know that none of the things he does is intentional, but because of a number of negative habits which has caused him to become callous, and sometimes even verbally cruel, prevents him from temporarily being the son I raised and know still lives deep within him. Plus, God has not given up on him, why should I? That question does not need to be answered, because for me and parents like me, there is no way we would ever give up on something we birthed into this world, and could, although not acknowledged, be the source of their failure to see the pain they cause us, simply because of the way we raised them.

Our Lord and Savior Jesus Christ was and is the perfect example of how we are to forgive the mean, although most times unintentional, ways of our children when He asked of His Father that those who were so cruel to Him while on the cross be forgiven because "They knew not what they were doing." Luke 23:34

I really don't know if by putting my thoughts on paper, and opening myself up, thereby; exposing my vulnerability, has or will help me to cope with my perceived feeling of being rejected and abandoned by my children or what has or will be accomplished by this effort, but it is a step in the right direction, not only for me personally but hopefully for the many parents out there that are going through the same predicament not really knowing how to make their painful and confusing situation better.

My solution for this phenomenon has been consistent throughout this work, and that is to let go and let God handle my every care, worry or concern. He and He alone can heal any and every wound we ourselves or man can inflict on us, when and only if we allow Him to do so.

My mind and heart keeps returning to my mother, and although I live almost a two-hour drive from our old home, I am still "drawn" to go by the old place just to reminisce about the "good old days". The house is now torn down and the acreage has sadly grown up in weeds from obvious abandonment, with sizable trees that were once tiny saplings, which was all over the place while we were growing-up there. Everything in nature, a clump of weeds, one blade upon another creating massive amounts of undergrowth, cattails that have been swallowed up by what once were saplings now trees, seems to have merged now that the house is no longer there to separate the living space from the "back forty".

The little stream which really was a ditch foaming with smelly stagnated water, teeming with mosquitoes, flies, spiders, creepy little worms and insects that I can't name, made their homes in this wet, oil covered habitat that was supposedly bubbling over from the underground oil vein my mother believed was there has all but disappeared as well. While I can still see the place where we kids had our "big business" in the form of a sparsely supplied vegetables and fruits stand, a venture we were certain would deliver us from the extreme poverty we suffered right after my step-dad died, is vivid in my mind's eye. Isn't it funny how just revisiting a place occupied in our childhood can bring back memories that were almost forgotten until you reflect on your past?

I still can see my mother and the way she was sitting that day in front of her home, with an air of sadness that even now, is suffocating, and my heart breaks because now I know and understand the separation anxieties she felt, realizing finally that we raise our children to become productive, God-fearing individuals, hopefully equipped with the knowledge and fortitude to withstand the many trials that life ultimately has waiting for them.

On the other hand, we also raise them, praying that they will grow-up without becoming so self-absorbed in their own lives that they forget, as I sadly did, that once gone, our mothers (and fathers) never come this way again.

In retrospect, it is also to our great disservice and most times ignorance that we often equate our life partners, or they should be, with that of a mother. By this I mean that we believe that our life partners will be with us until death, and will love us unconditionally as our mothers (and fathers) have, but realistically as previously stated, the divorce rate speaks differently. We, unfortunately, or at least some of us whether through divorce or death, have had more than one "life" mate, but sadly once a mother or in my case, a grandmother as well is gone, they cannot be replaced by anyone.

I apologize for not expressing the same sentiment when fathers are gone, but in a lot of families the fathers are dolefully, most times not intentionally; detached emotionally or worse yet, not physically there for the children to begin with especially and sadly this is more prevalent in African American homes. For those wonderful, God-fearing fathers that are there for their children, we have to recognize their presence and thank God for them. Not only are they the example the Lord has set forth for the rearing of his children, but also the Christian foundation needed to instill values and Christian morals in their children.

It would be so wonderful if all children had a dad in the home to nurture them and show them what it means to be a God-fearing husband and father, helping them to emulate fatherhood learned from example, not from wishing they had a father like "Tommy's" especially for male children. No matter how we look at it or what our personal experiences were with our father whether they were strong father figures, is what's sadly missing in society's interpretation of the ideal family.

Just think of how many young men and women that would not have encountered the snares of the enemy if they had been brought up in a positive and loving environment by both mother and father. I did not say bringing up children by a two mothers or two fathers household, taking on the role that God intended for male and female within the bounds of holy matrimony, those parental alternatives are clearly viewed as an abomination in God's sight. Some might counter with, isn't it better for a child to be brought up in a loving, two parent household regardless of the gender of those parents? As Christians, we know the answer.

But then, on the other hand, we must be fair to both sides of the God mandated parental team of male and female, because no matter what our personal opinion about any given situation might be, we have to acknowledge that there are always two sides to every situation. We could be very opinionated by saying there is no excuse for either parent to neglect their duties as parents, but death, divorce or the mother never being married sometimes causes this situation, but we still say in our opinionated judgment that nothing short of death should cause a child to be brought up without both parents. I would be very careful when taking such an opinionated stance because we will find ourselves dangerously close to judging someone, when it is not our Christian right to do so.

While children benefit the most from God fearing two parent homes, there are always those homes where physical, sexual and emotional abuse, abound. This is not to say that fathers are the primary perpetrators of these kinds of abuse, because in some instances, mothers have been equally guilty of abusing their children just as violently as fathers have, but the occurrence rate of abuse by a mother drops significantly when less stress is present, whether in a one or two parent family unit. This is the other darker reason a child will be brought up by only one parent, and thank God this horror is not experienced by every child being brought up in a single-parent home.

Again, for all the wonderful marriages that have lasted until one of the partners have died, I personally salute you, for you have truly been shown favor from God as a reward for all the hard work it takes to make a marriage work. You will be continually blessed for honoring the institution of marriage in the way the Lord has ordained the marriage vows to be kept. But, I have to say that the same integrity and love involved in keeping those marriages together, should also allow you to honor your parents in the same way God commanded of you when He said "Hearken unto thy father that begat thee, *and despise not thy mother when she is old.*" Proverbs 23:22

Looking back, I am now aware that we oft-times try to place blame on our children for not being the loving, considerate, and all giving creatures we want them to be, when in reality we should accept the fact that we are no less hurt or disillusioned than our parents before us were, they just had a better way of dealing with this not so pleasant situation. I am also reminded, with both remorse and embarrassment at how I placed everything before the needs of my dying mother and grandmother only to come to this juncture in life when I know that *all* of our priorities are sadly misdirected when we fail to balance the needs of *all* those we profess to love with those of our own.

Do you suppose the blinders we place on ourselves gives us license to think of ourselves first no matter what the screaming, warning signs are telling us when someone we profess to love needs us? Does it really make us feel better or do we just go on blindly thinking our behavior is what everyone else is doing? Too bad, because when the blinders come off, we are stuck with the fact that we are no better than the heathen when it comes to understanding the needs of those we profess to love. May God have mercy on all of us?

Chapter Twenty-Six: Resolution

Ralph Waldo Emerson captured the essence of both my mother and grandmother in his poem "The House". The verses in this poem, encapsulates the qualities these dynamic women shared which enabled them to build their "houses" of moral fortitude that is present in the lives of all us kids. I will go one step further by saying not only did these women give me what I consider to be the greatest gift imaginable, but a gift that is transcendent. The only greater gift is God's gift of salvation, both being crucial in my abilities to make a difference in the lives of all I meet.

The common and continuous thread throughout this work has been to inform you of the sustaining love and grace given to us by our Lord and Savior Jesus Christ. He (Jesus) helped my mother and my grandmother live through the hardships and disappointments experienced while raising us kids, and this same innate, God inspired love and grace continues to buffer the pain that I'm experiencing while trying to make sense of my relationship with my kids, specifically the perceptions of being abandoned and put out to pasture by my adult children way before I feel that I am ready.

I know without doubt that it is God and His unfailing love and wisdom that will ultimately help us all successfully reach the finish line, in spite of the insurmountable obstacles we face whether perceived or real when it comes to understanding and dealing with the less than caring attitudes displayed by our adult children. I thank and praise Him daily for this wonderful gift of comfort and love. But the most important and greatest of these gifts from God is His Grace *and* Salvation.

I will conclude this labor of love by quoting Mr. Emerson's poem in its entirety with the desire and prayer that all I've shared with you will somehow help you to see yourself as a conqueror of a very painful situation, but more importantly, I want you to know that you are a child of God, a child that God has promised He will never leave or forsake.

It is also my prayer that all adult children will read this attempt to shed light on a subject that is very painful to many parents that feel abandoned by their children, and that it will in many ways help adult children that are less than charitable when it comes to the often times perceived ideas that a parent is just getting old and seeking or demanding attention, will make them step back and reflect. May God Bless and keep each and every one that has allowed me to share my pain, my confusion, my joy, and finally, my resolve with them.

A Mother's Prayer

Heavenly Father,

Thank you for blessing me with the gift of four beautiful children. I know I have not been the example **You** would have me to be as a mother, but I also know that Your love, compassion, and forgiveness takes all of our frailties and failures into consideration. Teach us Father by Your example how to be Godly parents, raising children that will first honor **Your** name and Godhood and then to honor us as mothers and parents.

Teach our children, by our example, to in turn instruct our children in all **Your** ways so that they will be able to show the compassion, love, and patience required to be a blessing to their parents. Father, we know that all our efforts as parents are to be modeled after **You** and **Your** examples, so please Father, give us what it takes to not only raise our children in a Godly manner, but to also teach them how to love and honor us when we are old.

Amen

The House

By: Ralph Waldo Emerson

There is no architect
Can build as the muse can;
She is skillful to select
Materials of the plan;

Slow and warily to choose
Rafters of immortal pine,
Or cedar incorruptible,
Worthy her design.

She treads dark Alpine forests,
Or valleys by the sea,
In many lands, with painful steps,
Ere she can find a tree.

NEVER THIS WAY AGAIN

She ransacks mines and ledges,
And quarries every rock,
To hew the famous adamant,
For each eternal block.

She lays her beams in music,
In music every one,
To the cadence of the whirling world
Which dances round the sun?

That so they shall not be displaced
By lapses or by wars,
But for the love of happy souls
Outlive the newest stars.

"She looketh well to the ways of her household, and eateth not the bread of idleness. Her children arise up, and call her blessed;" Proverbs 31:27-28.

"God could not be everywhere, so He created mothers." – Jewish Proverb

The End

www.ingramcontent.com/pod-product-compliance
Lightning Source LLC
Chambersburg PA
CBHW071331110526
44591CB00010B/1105